KU-331-981

This book is to be returned on or before
the last date stamped below.

100 GREATEST

SPORTS CHAMPIONS

NEWCASTLE-UNDER-LYME
COLLEGE LIBRARY

Donald Sommerville

DRAGON'S WORLD

Newcastle under Lyme College

DC017618

DRAGON'S WORLD

CHILDREN'S BOOKS

Dragon's World Ltd
London House
Great Eastern Wharf
Parkgate Road
London
SW11 4NQ

First published by Dragon's World Ltd, 1997

© Dragon's World Ltd, 1997

No part of this book may be reproduced
or transmitted in any form or by any
means, electronic or mechanical, including
photocopy, recording, or any information
storage and retrieval system, without
permission in writing from Dragon's
World Limited, except by a reviewer who
may quote brief passages in a review.

All rights reserved.

British Library
Cataloguing in Publication Data
The catalogue record for this book is
available from the British Library.

ISBN 1 85028 315 X

Editor: Diana Briscoe
Picture Researcher: Richard Philpott
Designer: Mel Raymond
Art Director: John Strange
Design Assistants: Karen Ferguson
                    Victoria Furbisher
DTP Manager: Michael Burgess
Editorial Director: Pippa Rubinstein

Typeset by Dragon's World Ltd
in Stempel Garamond and Gill

Printed in Italy

Contents

796.092 SOM

NEWCASTLE-UNDER-LYME
COLLEGE LIBRARY
DC017618

Introduction

Sports come in many different forms and the stories of the champions of sport are as varied, unusual and interesting as the games they play.

This book includes a range of past and present champions from many of the most popular sports played around the world. All have some special quality attached to them. Perhaps they qualify as all-time-greats in their sport because of a long list of world records, or perhaps they are best known for a single outstanding achievement, or for having got where they did against the odds and by overcoming problems and disadvantages.

Great sporting champions come in all shapes and sizes and nationalities.

The smallest and lightest of the champions in this book is probably Nadia Comaneci, whose grace and agility stunned the whole world and not just fans of her sport of gymnastics. What could be more different from that than the power and weight of Taiho, the greatest-ever sumo wrestler?

It is easy to see that the basketball players in our book are very tall and that the long-distance runners and cyclists tend to be thin and wiry, but it is far harder to say just what made these very different people into champions.

When you look closely at them all you find that they do have much in common despite their very different

skills and backgrounds. Jack Nicklaus played golf well almost as soon as he started, but then he practised hard throughout the time he was growing up. Then he found inside himself the desire to win, and the ability to keep playing well under the fierce pressure of top-level competitions. Every one of the champions in this book could tell the same story in a slightly different way.

It is impossible to say whether a champion in one sport is 'better' than a champion in another, but what we can say is that all the men, women and teams in this book have pleased millions of fans throughout the world and that we can have fun finding out some more about them, too.

DONALD SOMMERVILLE

OPPOSITE TOP LEFT: Jim Thorpe (American football)
TOP RIGHT: Bonnie Blair (ice skating)
BELOW: Don Bradman batting (cricket)

TOP: Nikolai Andrianov (gymnastics)
BELOW: Matti Nykänen (skiing)

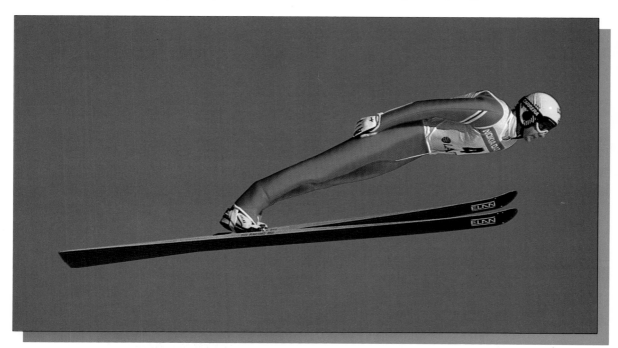

7

Jim Brown

USA, born 1936

Jim Brown was the best fullback ever to play American football, but some people think that this may not even have been his best sport. He played basketball at college and competed at top level in the decathlon, but lacrosse fans think he may have been the best all-round player ever in their game.

After twice being named All-American in college football, Brown was drafted in 1957 by the Cleveland Browns. He made Rookie of the Year and, in his second year (1958), set an incredible new record for rushing yards gained in the season, improving the old mark by more than one-third. In his nine-year professional career, he led the league in rushing eight times, 'failing' only in 1962, and never missed a single game because of injury.

The records he set are gradually being beaten by modern stars because of changes in the way the game is played. Even so, his career rushing yards total of 12,312 yards was only surpassed by Walter Payton in the 1980s. Brown's average gain per carry of the ball was 5.2 yards and this has yet to be beaten.

Fact File

Jim Brown: 1.85 m, 106 kg
Syracuse University: All-American
National Football League career: 1957–65
Rushing record: 12,312 yards (average 5.2 yards),
    106 touchdowns
Receiving: 2,499 yards (average 9.5 yards), twenty
    touchdowns

▶ To commemorate Jim Brown's achievements the Cleveland Browns retired his number 32 when he finished playing.

Joe Montana
USA, born 1956

Joe Montana was one of the greatest quarterbacks ever to play American football. Montana began his big-time career with the Fighting Irish of Notre Dame, always one of the strongest of the US college teams. His most famous game there was the 1979 Cotton Bowl, when he led the team from 34–12 down in the third quarter to a 35–34 win.

The scouts for the professional teams of the NFL thought he might be rather inconsistent, so he was only picked, or drafted, by the San Francisco 49'ers in the third round, but he soon won a place in their starting line up.

Overall, San Francisco were probably the strongest team in the NFL in the 1980s – thanks largely to Montana's leadership on the field. Montana soon became known as the most accurate

▲ Montana as a Kansas City Chief.

A great quarterback needs to be matched with a great pass receiver if his talents are to be fully recognized. Montana's favourite partner for the second half of his career at San Francisco was Jerry Rice, perhaps the greatest wide receiver of all time.

passing quarterback in the game with an uncanny ability to inspire his team to make great come-backs from apparently hopeless situations. Montana led the 49'ers in four Super Bowl wins (1982, 1985, 1989 and 1990). Montana missed most of the 1991 and 1992 seasons because of injury. He retired in 1995 after two seasons with the Kansas City Chiefs.

◀ Montana in action in Super Bowl XXIII. The 49'ers beat the Bengals 20-16.

Joe Namath
USA, born 1943

Joe Namath is famed particularly for the great game at Super Bowl III (played on 12 January 1969), when he led the New York Jets to a stunning underdog victory over the powerful Baltimore Colts. Namath was chosen as the game's 'most valuable player' (MVP) after this upset 16–7 win for the Jets.

Namath had joined the professional ranks in 1965 from the University of Alabama. He signed up for the Jets for US $400,000, and quickly began to justify what was then a huge sum. In his first season, he passed for over 2,000 yards and was chosen as Rookie of the Year. In 1967 he became the first professional quarterback to pass for more than 4,000 yards in a season; in 1968 he was chosen as his league's MVP.

▲ Joe Namath doing what he did best, making a big passing play, this time in a pre-season Jets-Giants game in 1969.

The AFL and the NFL
When Joe Namath became a professional footballer, two formerly rival leagues in American football, the American Football League (AFL) and the National Football League (NFL), had only recently joined together. The Jets were an AFL team and their win in Super Bowl III was the first ever by an AFL team.

Above all, Namath liked to pass the football. He probably had the strongest arm of any quarterback in football history, and he relished the challenge of going for the big plays. Touchdowns were his target, and he passed for 173 touchdowns in his professional career. Although he was hampered in the later years of his career by knee injuries, he played on until 1977 eventually gaining 27,663 yards as a passer from 1,886 pass completions.

◀ Joe Namath's great talent was recognized when he was elected to the Pro Football Hall of Fame in 1985.

Jim Thorpe
USA, 1888–1953

Jim Thorpe is the only man ever to have won both the decathlon and the pentathlon at the Olympic Games – a feat that will never be repeated. This triumph came in the 1912 Olympics held at Stockholm in Sweden. To make these wins even more impressive, he set world records in both events. A year later his gold medals were taken away because he had been paid US $15 a week for playing baseball earlier in his career, and being paid for playing any sport was then against the rules of track and field.

Thorpe's ancestry was part native American and his college was Carlisle Indian School, where he was coached by one of American football's greatest coaches, Pop Warner. Thorpe was a football All-American in 1911 and 1912 at college, as well as starring at track and

Jim Thorpe's Olympic Medals
Jim Thorpe's family never stopped thinking that his medals had been taken away unfairly. Finally, in 1982, the International Olympic Committee agreed, and one of Thorpe's daughters was presented with replicas of the trophies which her father had deservedly won seventy years before.

field. From 1913 to 1919, he played pro baseball for the New York Giants, Boston Braves and Cincinnati Reds.

He also played professional football with the Canton Bulldogs, one of the top teams at that time. In 1920, he helped the Bulldogs join a new football league that eventually became the forerunner of the modern NFL. The Bulldogs became the Cleveland Indians in 1921 and Thorpe played with them and other teams until his career ended with the Chicago Cardinals in 1928.

▲◀ Jim Thorpe was one of the truly great and truly versatile athletes. Here he is seen (top) with the New York Giants and (left) with the Canton Bulldogs.

Hank Aaron
USA, born 1934

For many years, one of baseball's most sacred records was the lifetime total of 714 home runs established by the great Babe Ruth, but all records are passed eventually. The man who beat Babe Ruth's total was Henry 'Hammerin' Hank' Aaron with a new mark of 755.

Aaron played for most of his career with the Braves, starting with them in Milwaukee in 1954 and moving with the team to Atlanta in 1966. Aaron's finest moment came in front of his own fans in Atlanta in April 1974 when he hit his 715th home run, off Al Downing of the Los Angeles Dodgers.

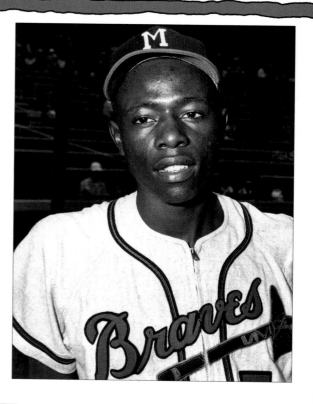

Aaron never beat fifty 'homers' in a season, but he was always consistent. His lifetime hitting average was a very fine .305, and he was also a top-class rightfielder. He combined all this with a modest off-the-field personality that brought him a host of fans. However, as one of the first black players to star in baseball, he also met with racial prejudice, especially early on.

Fact File

Professional career: 1954–76
Clubs: Milwaukee (later Atlanta) Braves, Milwaukee Brewers
Career statistics: 3,771 hits, average .305, 755 home runs, 2,297 runs batted in

◀ 8 April 1974 and Hank Aaron watches his 715th record-breaking home run sail over the fence. Al Downing of the Dodgers was the unfortunate pitcher.

Joe DiMaggio
USA, born 1914

Joe DiMaggio was the leading player of the New York Yankees when the team dominated American baseball in the 1930s and 1940s. Known as 'Joltin' Joe' for his powerful hitting, DiMaggio joined the Yankees in 1936 and it was no accident that the club then won four World Series titles in a row. He played for the Yankees throughout his professional career (1936–51).

DiMaggio's most lasting personal achievement came in 1941 when he made at least one base hit in 56 consecutive games, a record that still stands unbeaten. After ending his run with a failure against the Cleveland Indians, DiMaggio then had another sixteen-game streak – an achievement in its own right. DiMaggio played at centerfield and was also a star on his team's defence. It was said that he did not make a single error as a base runner in his whole career.

Joe DiMaggio finished his career with a .325 batting average and 361 home runs, and his slugging average of .579 stands sixth on the all-time list. In 1954, he was back in the headlines when he married and then divorced the famous movie star Marilyn Monroe.

▲ Joe DiMaggio at spring training.
▼ DiMaggio makes another hit during his great spell in the 1941 season.

Hideo Nomo
Japan, born 1968

Baseball has traditionally been regarded as the USA's number one favourite sport, with US players and leagues considered the best in the world. However, baseball has gradually spread into Central and Southern America and across the Pacific Ocean, and now a Japanese player is making US players and fans sit up and take notice.

Hideo Nomo began pitching in Japan's top league in 1990 with the Kintetsu Buffaloes, and immediately proved that he would become a major star. He was not only acclaimed Rookie of the Year, but also added the prizes for best pitcher and most valuable player!

Sadaharu Oh
Nomo may develop into Japan's finest pitcher, but there is no doubt who was Japan's finest hitter. Sadaharu Oh (born 1940) led the Japan League in home runs fifteen times, hitting 868 in his 22-year career with the Yomiuri Giants. The US record is Hank Aaron's 755.

In the first four seasons he had with Kintetsu, he was top of the league figures for games won, strikeouts and earned-run average. Then he decided to try his luck in the USA, signing with the Los Angeles Dodgers. American baseball was looking for a new star in 1995 after the players' strike of 1994, and Nomo was the man. His pitching was so impressive that he made selection for the All-Star game in his first season. Even the best US stars were bewildered by his unusual, twisting, pitching action and the lightning-fast fastball that he produced.

◄ Hideo Nomo has an unusual pitching style producing an extremely fierce fastball.

Jackie Robinson
USA, 1919–72

When Jackie Robinson stepped out for the first time with the Brooklyn Dodgers in April 1947, he was the first black player to appear regularly with any of baseball's top teams. Robinson attended the University of California at Los Angeles before World War II, and was a star of American football, baseball, basketball, and track and field (he was one of the world's best long-jumpers).

In 1946, he was signed by the Brooklyn Dodgers, and made his major league debut a year later. Robinson had great strength of character, and this, together with his great playing skills, helped him in his fight against the racism that he encountered.

▲ Jackie Robinson during a season he spent with Montreal in the minor leagues before his breakthrough with the Dodgers.

▼ Jackie Robinson uses all his speed to slide safely into home base during a 1952 match with the Chicago Cubs. Robinson put his athletic talents to effective use as an outfielder as well.

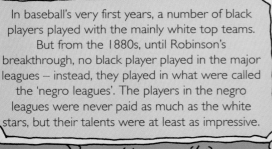

In baseball's very first years, a number of black players played with the mainly white top teams. But from the 1880s, until Robinson's breakthrough, no black player played in the major leagues – instead, they played in what were called the 'negro leagues'. The players in the negro leagues were never paid as much as the white stars, but their talents were at least as impressive.

'Babe' Ruth

USA, 1895–1948

Babe Ruth may have been baseball's finest-ever player. Some of his records have been beaten in more recent years, but no one has come near his lifetime slugging average of .690. No other player has hit fifty home runs in more than two seasons – 'the Babe' managed this four times. Most impressive of all, he hit home runs 8.5 per cent of his times at bat.

George Herman Ruth started being called 'the Babe' early on when he played for the Boston Red Sox. He had success as a pitcher with Boston, as well as batting powerfully. He was traded to the New York Yankees in 1920. In his first season there he hit an amazing 54 home runs and soon switched to playing rightfield. He stayed with the Yankees, then baseball's strongest team, for most of his career which ran from 1914 to 1935.

▶ Babe Ruth practising with the Boston Braves at the end of his career.

▼ Babe Ruth brought so many fans to baseball that Yankee Stadium was called 'the house that Ruth built'.

Babe Ruth hit baseball's most famous home run in the 1932 World Series. Coming up to bat for the Yankees in the third game, Ruth pointed at the farthest part of the fence, allowed two strikes to go past, then blasted the next into the crowd, exactly where he had shown he would.

Cy Young
USA, 1867–1955

Cy Young played as a pitcher for the unfancied Boston Red Sox in the first-ever World Series in 1903. During what was then a nine-game series, he won two games and helped his club to a shock 5–3 win. Young, whose full name was Denton True Young, is remembered for much more than the part he played in the famous 1903 World Series.

From 1890 to 1911, he played with the Cleveland Spiders, St Louis Cardinals, Boston Red Sox and Cleveland Indians. In his remarkable career, he won 511 games, by a long way

Professional baseball's two top leagues in north America are the National League (founded 1876) and the American League (founded 1901). The annual championship between the two leagues, called the World Series, was first played in 1903.

the best total ever. Only one other pitcher has won more than 400 games and no current player is near 300.

It is sometimes pointed out that Young lost more games than any other pitcher in the history of baseball – but his long career undoubtedly contributed to this fact. However, his game was consistently good: he won more than twenty games in twenty of his twenty-two seasons, and more than thirty games in five of the twenty seasons. With this record it is appropriate that the trophies awarded every year for the best pitchers in the two American baseball leagues are still known as the Cy Young awards.

◀ Cy Young warms up his pitching arm before another match in his long and successful career.

Kareem Abdul-Jabbar
USA, born 1947

Kareem Abdul-Jabbar was one of the best centres ever to play the game. His trademark shot was his famous 'sky hook', with which he won points from long range.

After starring in high school basketball in New York, Lew Alcindor, as he was then known, went on to UCLA and helped them win three consecutive NCAA championships.

Next, he was drafted by the Milwaukee Bucks, a weak team, made them title contenders in his first year and led them to the NBA championship in 1972. During this period he became a Muslim and changed his name. In 1976, Abdul-Jabbar moved to the Los Angeles Lakers and played there until 1989, winning the NBA title with the team five times.

Fact File
Height: 2.18 m
Points scored: 38,387 (5,762 in play-offs) – both
  best ever
Career points average: 24.6
MVP: 1971, 1972, 1974, 1976, 1977, 1980
All-American (UCLA): 1967–9

▼ Kareem Abdul-Jabbar in points scoring action in the familiar yellow uniform of the Los Angeles Lakers.

Larry Bird
USA, born 1956

His critics said he was slow around the court and could not jump very well, but Larry Bird was still one of the greatest basketball forwards ever. He was a brilliant passer of the ball and had that special ability that helped the rest of his team play to their full potential.

At college he played for Indiana State, not normally a top side, and led them into the NCAA finals in his senior year when he was also named All-American for the second time.

When he turned professional in 1980, he was selected, or drafted, by the Boston Celtics and played with them for the whole of his career until his retirement in 1992. His peak was in the middle of the 1980s. He was named the National Basketball Association's (NBA's) Most Valuable Player in 1984 and 1986, and helped the Celtics to NBA championships in both of those years.

▲ Larry Bird scored 21,791 points for the Celtics in the course of his great career.

The 'Dream Team'
For the first time in 1992, the US Olympic basketball team was selected from the finest professional players in the NBA. Superstars, such as Michael Jordan and Magic Johnson, were in the team but Larry Bird was voted in as captain. The 'Dream Team' won the gold medal, and after this success, Bird retired.

Bird was brought up in a small Indiana town called French Lick, and became known as 'the hick from French Lick' ('hick' means 'yokel'). Away from the basketball court, Bird remained a country boy at heart, but on court he had class and technique to spare.

◀ Larry Bird makes a drive for the basket, leaving an opponent stranded behind him.

Chicago Bulls
USA, founded 1966

Before the mid-1980s, the Chicago Bulls had been one of the National Basketball Association's least successful teams. That began to change when they drafted Michael Jordan in 1983. Almost from the start, Jordan was a scoring sensation and the Bulls began to look like winners.

Real success began in 1991 when the Los Angeles Lakers were defeated 4–1 in the finals to give Chicago their first title. Repeat wins in 1992 over Portland and over Phoenix in 1993 showed that a basketball dynasty to rival the great teams of the past was being founded.

Then Jordan said that he was leaving to play baseball, and the Bulls slumped.

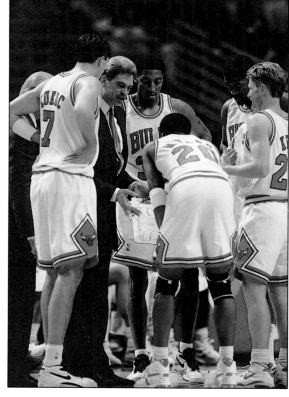

▲ Chicago coach Phil Jackson has one of the best records of any NBA coach ever.

In 1994 Jordan returned and in 1995 the Bulls reached the playoffs again.

▼ Muscle stretching is a vital part of athletic preparation as these Bulls show.

Winners in the NBA
The Chicago Bulls have a long way to go before their total of title wins catches up with basketball's most famous team of all, the Boston Celtics. The Celtics have won the championship sixteen times, including a period from 1957 to 1969 when they won eleven times in thirteen years.

Michael Jordan
USA, born 1963

Michael Jordan is the greatest modern basketball player and probably the richest – he promotes many different sports products, especially for the Nike shoe company. Jordan was a noted player in college at North Carolina and a member of the 1984 US Olympic gold-medal team. He was only taken as the third choice in the draft of players into the NBA, but once with the Chicago Bulls he almost instantly won recognition as the league's best scorer.

His points total in his first season (2,313) was the highest in the NBA, but his average let him down. After missing most of the next season with injury he won his first of seven successive scoring titles in 1986. Jordan's trademark was an ability seemingly to hang in the air and defy gravity, and he soon became known as 'His Airness' to his many fans.

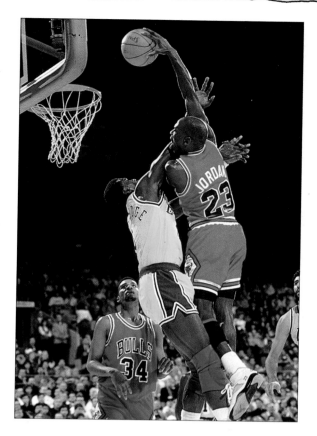

▲ The Lakers' defence cannot stop Jordan making another basket in the 1989–90 season.

From 1987 until 1993, he kept breaking records: highest career scoring average (32.3 points per game), most valuable player three times, defensive player of the year once and, best of all, gained three NBA titles with the Bulls from 1991 to 1993.

In 1993 Jordan gave up basketball for more than a year in an unsuccessful attempt to develop a second career as a baseball player. He came back to basketball for the 1994–5 season and could not quite recapture his old form, but who knows what he can still achieve?

◄ Michael Jordan takes to the air in another scoring demonstration of his uncanny leaping ability.

Magic Johnson
USA, born 1959

Earvin 'Magic' Johnson was one of basketball's greatest stars throughout the 1980s. He joined the Los Angeles Lakers from the Michigan State Spartans in 1979, and soon showed the fans what he could do.

In his first season in 1980, he played in the NBA finals, and in the sixth and last game he played centre instead of his usual position of point guard because Kareem Abdul-Jabbar was injured. Magic Johnson scored an astonishing forty-two points, fifteen rebounds and seven assists, and walked off the court with the play-offs' most valued player (MVP) award.

Johnson was unusually tall for a guard at 2.06 m, but had great handling and passing skills. His performance in his first title series was one of many when he proved that he had the versatility to play in positions other than point guard. Throughout his career he played with the Lakers, who were the best team in the basketball league in the 1980s, winning the NBA title five times and being finalists on three more occasions.

▲ Magic Johnson uses all his agility to get in a shot.

Shortly before the start of the NBA season in 1991, Magic Johnson announced that he was retiring from the game and that he had been infected with HIV, the virus that leads to the disease, AIDS. However, he played for the US 'Dream Team' in the 1992 Olympics, and since then has put his great popularity to work in the campaign against AIDS.

Magic Johnson was named as NBA MVP three times, in 1987, 1989 and 1990. His career total of 9,921 assists is the best ever, and shows that he was, above all, the sort of player who made his team play better.

◀ Magic Johnson celebrates the USA's 1992 Olympic basketball gold medal.

Cheryl Miller
USA, born 1964

Cheryl Miller was the best female basketball player ever. Her list of awards and records is almost endless. Most of her notable achievements were as a college player with the University of Southern California. She led the team there to two US national titles in 1983 and 1984, and was selected as the top player of the NCAA Final Four tournament in both of those winning years.

She won women's basketball's top trophy, the Naismith Award for the best player of the season, an unheard of three years in a row (1984–6), and in 1984 was voted as Collegiate Woman Athlete of the Year.

▲ The USC cheerleaders look on in admiration as Cheryl Miller demonstrates her skills.

▼ Cheryl Miller has no trouble rising above the hoop in this picture of her taken during a practice routine.

Cheryl Miller is not the only top basketball player in her family. Her brother, Reggie Miller, is one of the stars of the NBA Indiana Pacers. He has not achieved the success of his sister, but is regularly his team's top scorer, and led the Pacers to the Eastern Conference Final in the play-offs in 1994.

In 1984 she played for the US Olympic women's basketball team in the Olympic Games at Los Angeles. She was the star of the side which won the gold medal. She played for other US national teams in 1986, as well as becoming first draft choice for a new professional women's basketball league. (This league was not a financial success and soon came to an end.) Cheryl Miller hoped to make the US Olympic team in 1988, but injury brought her retirement.

Hakeem Olajuwon
Nigeria/USA, born 1963

Hakeem Olajuwon is not the most outspoken of the current top basketball players, but he may be the best of the lot, now that Michael Jordan is no longer at his brilliant best. Nigerian by birth, he became a college star in the USA. He was selected as All-American in 1984 and had been named MVP in the Final Four college tournament in 1983. It was no surprise he was the number one draft choice for the NBA in 1984 when he joined the Houston Rockets.

Olajuwon began to repay the Rockets' faith in him from his very first season when he was elected Rookie of the Year. He has been named to the All-NBA first team five times, the first being in 1987,

▶ Olajuwon jumps to shoot against the Pacers.

▼ Playing in a match early in 1995.

Fact File
Olajuwon's NBA titles
Rookie of the Year: 1984
Regular season MVP: 1994
Defensive Player of the Year: 1993, 1994
Top rebounder: 1989, 1990
Top shot blocker: 1990, 1991, 1993

but even better was to come in 1994 and 1995 when he led the unfancied Rockets to consecutive NBA titles.

In 1994, Olajuwon and his team beat the New York Knicks 4–3, and in 1995 they did it again the hard way. The Rockets came into the playoffs seeded only fifth after a modest season, but recaptured their best play to gain a finals place against Shaquille O'Neal's Orlando Magic. The confrontation between the NBA's two premier teams was one sided, for Olajuwon and the Rockets ran away with the title 4–0.

Shaquille O'Neal
USA, born 1972

As one of the superstars of the modern game of basketball, Shaquille O'Neal has a seven-year contract with the Orlando Magic which is worth US $42,000,000.

O'Neal joined the Orlando Magic in the 1992 NBA draft after being twice selected as All-American in college. O'Neal's great scoring ability won him the award as NBA Rookie of the Year in 1993. In 1995, he finally gained his first top spot in the scoring table.

O'Neal's great weakness is his free throw shooting. With a good free throw percentage, O'Neal would be far ahead in the scoring tables.

O'Neal is one of the best-known NBA stars for his off-court activities, but he also has the respect of the other stars. This was demonstrated when he was picked as part of the USA's 'Dream Team II', which won the 1994 World Championship (see page 19).

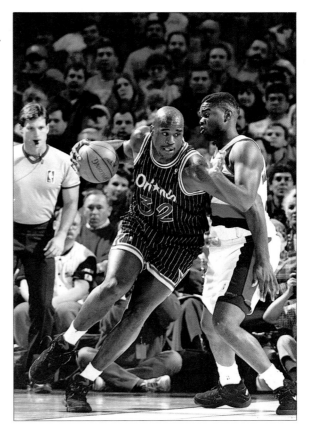

▼ Shaquille O'Neal is a massive man. His playing position is centre and he is 2.15 m tall and weighs 138 kg.

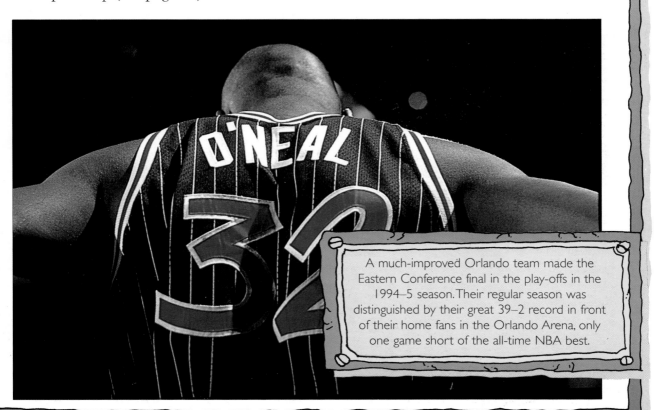

A much-improved Orlando team made the Eastern Conference final in the play-offs in the 1994–5 season. Their regular season was distinguished by their great 39–2 record in front of their home fans in the Orlando Arena, only one game short of the all-time NBA best.

Jeanne Longo
France, born 1958

Jeanne Longo is regarded as the finest all-round woman cycle racer ever. She was world road race champion from 1985 to 1987 and in 1989, pursuit champion in 1986, 1988 and 1989, and won the points title in 1989. In addition to these successes, she held both the road race and pursuit championships unbeaten from 1980 to 1989 in her home country of France. If she had any weakness it was in her sprinting speed.

Some cycling records are set with the help of a motorcycle – the cyclist rides close behind, which helps the rider to go at the correct pace – but the true records are set alone and from a standing start. In 1989, Longo established unaided records for 3 kilometres and one hour which are still unbeaten. Set at altitude in Mexico, her 1-hour ride was an astonishing 46.35 km.

▲ Jeanne Longo during a pursuit race competition.

Her other successes include wins in the women's Tour de France in 1987, 1988 and 1989, and a silver medal in the road race at the 1992 Olympics.

▼ Longo in the yellow jersey of the race leader during the 1987 Tour de France which she won.

Chris Boardman
Great Britain, born 1968

Chris Boardman was already competing at the top before he was out of his teens.

By the 1992 Olympics, Boardman's speciality had become the 4,000 metres individual pursuit race, and he had a revolutionary new bicycle, partly produced by Lotus, the famous racing car maker. Boardman won the gold medal, defeating his opponent in the final by a huge margin.

Boardman turned professional in 1994 and won the 42 kilometres time trial in the World Road Race Championships to add to the world one-hour distance record that he held in 1993 to 1994.

▲ Boardman at the 1994 World Championships.

Like most first-time competitors in the Tour de France, Boardman dropped out well before the end in 1994. Unlike most first-timers, he won the prologue time trial and gained the right to wear the famous yellow jersey, holding it for three days in which the Tour de France was racing in England. In 1995, Boardman was badly injured and eliminated during the prologue stage.

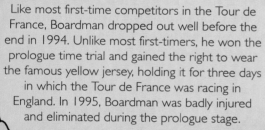

He made his debut in the Tour de France in 1994, and success in this race remains his great ambition.

▼ Boardman on one of the new super high-tech bikes that have revolutionized cycle racing.

Miguel Indurain
Spain, born 1964

The Tour de France is the toughest race in the cycling world and one of the hardest in all sport. Miguel Indurain is the only person who has won it five years in succession (1991–95).

Indurain is not a great sprinter, but he is the finest time-trialler of his generation, building up huge leads over his opponents in these sections. Then he defends his times with astonishing power and determination in the mountain stages, where so many riders have their challenges broken.

Indurain competed for Spain in the 1984 Olympics as an amateur before turning professional the next year. Like many other riders, he dropped out of the race in his first two entries in the Tour de France, but gradually moved up

▲ Miguel Indurain showing all his power and determination during an attempt on the world 1-hour distance record in September 1994.

the rankings after then. He recorded his first stage win in 1989 when he was seventeenth overall.

As well as his Tour de France wins, he has also won the important Giro d'Italia race twice, and holds the 1-hour world record of 53.04 km.

Each year as Indurain's reputation has grown the headlines in the cycling magazines have been, 'Can anyone catch Indurain?' The answer so far has been a definite 'no'.

Indurain's Remarkable Physique
Indurain is tall for a top cyclist (1.88 m), but is a very powerful rider. His lung capacity has been measured at eight litres, twice that of a normal healthy adult man, and his resting heart beat is 28 per minute (compared with about 68 for the average man).

◀ Indurain in the familiar race-leader's yellow jersey during the 1995 Tour de France. He is closely followed by one of his Banesto team-mates.

Eddy Merckx
Belgium, born 1945

In cycling's great races, the leaders in the various categories of competition wear a distinctive coloured jersey. Only Eddy Merckx has ever finished the Tour de France, entitled to wear all three leaders' jerseys as overall winner, points champion and 'King of the Mountains'.

Merckx and three others have each won the Tour de France five times, but Merckx stands alone with 35 stage wins and 96 days as race leader. Merckx's wins were in 1969–72 and 1974.

He also won the Giro d'Italia five times, and in 1974 was the first cyclist to win the three top races, the Tour de France, the Giro d'Italia and the world road race championship in the same year.

▲ Eddy Merckx in Tour de France action.

▼ Eddy Merckx crosses the finish line to win the 1971 world professional road race championship.

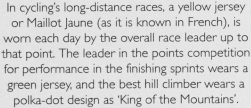

In cycling's long-distance races, a yellow jersey or Maillot Jaune (as it is known in French), is worn each day by the overall race leader up to that point. The leader in the points competition for performance in the finishing sprints wears a green jersey, and the best hill climber wears a polka-dot design as 'King of the Mountains'.

Ian Botham
Great Britain, born 1955

Ian Botham is considered to be England's best cricket all-rounder – his bold and aggressive style endeared him to the cricket fans.

English supporters began to think that someone special had been found on Botham's very first day in Test cricket against Australia in 1977 when he took five wickets. The next year, in a match against Pakistan, he became the first player to score a century and take eight wickets in a Test match – a feat that has not been equalled. He reached the double of 1,000 runs and 100 wickets in only twenty-one matches, quicker than anyone else had ever done.

His magnificent individual performances brought Botham the England captaincy in 1980 and 1981, but this was not a success and his form suffered. However, as soon as he resigned the captaincy, he was back to his

best with two astonishing centuries and match-winning bowling performances against Australia.

Botham's big-hitting batting style brought him a record eighty sixes in one season in 1985, and his total of 383 Test match wickets as a bowler set the record for a time, but has since been beaten.

Off the cricket field, Ian Botham put his fame to good use by walking the length of Britain from John O'Groats to Land's End in 1985 to raise money for charity.
In 1988, he followed in the footsteps of Hannibal, a famous general of the ancient world, and walked over the Alps with a group of elephants.

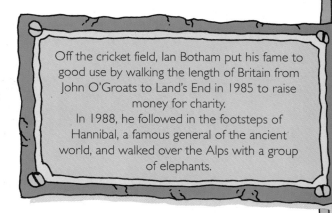

◀ Ian Botham demonstrates his strength and liking for the big hit that made him such a favourite with the fans.

Don Bradman
Australia, born 1908

Sir Donald Bradman's playing record leaves no doubt that he was the greatest cricket batsman ever. Only five players have a batting average of more than sixty in Test cricket. Four of these have figures of between 60 and 65. Bradman's final mark in his career for Australia was more than half as much again – 99.94 – and would have been over 100 if he had made only four runs in his last innings instead of being out for a duck (scored 0).

He was in the Australian team from 1928 until he retired in 1948/9. Bradman's most famous match was against England in 1930. He made 309 not out on the first day of the match and went on to a world record 334 runs that stood unbeaten for many years.

▼ The 'Little Master', as Bradman was known, plays a delicate scoring shot despite the attentions of England stars Godfrey Evans (left) and Bill Edrich.

Fact File

First-class career: 1927–49, New South Wales, later South Australia

Runs scored: 28,067 runs, average 95.14, 117 centuries, highest score 452 not out

Test matches: 52

Tests for Australia, 6,996 runs, average 99.94, 29 centuries, highest score 334

C.B. Fry
Great Britain, 1872–1956

Charles Burgess Fry competed to international standard in three sports, and was almost as good in several more. He was a fine example of a type of all-round sportsman who could not exist in the modern world.

He first made his mark as a long-jumper, setting a new world record in 1893 that remained unbeaten for over twenty years. In the winters, he found time to play rugby union at the top level, while at soccer he played for England in 1901 and in the FA Cup final with Southampton in 1902.

His best sport was cricket. He played first-class cricket for both Sussex and Hampshire at various times from 1892 to 1921, and in Test matches for England from 1892 to 1912.

Knowing his limitations did not only apply to his cricket. Away from sport, Fry had a notable career as an international diplomat. He was even offered the chance to become King of Albania, a country that had been formed in 1912, but he politely declined.

Fry made ninety-four centuries in his career, and in his best season in 1901 he scored six hundreds in successive innings. He based his technique on a limited range of strokes, but he had the concentration and self-discipline to play them supremely well.

◀ No batting helmets or thigh padding in C.B. Fry's day!

Rachel Heyhoe-Flint
Great Britain, born 1939

Rachel Heyhoe-Flint was best known for her contribution to raising the public profile of women's cricket – through her work she brought commercial interest and sponsorship to the game.

Heyhoe-Flint was far more than just a good publicist for her sport. She remains at the top of the list of run-scorers in women's Test matches with 1,814 runs at an average of just over forty-nine from her twenty-five appearances – the sort of figures that most men would be very pleased with indeed.

She had success in one-day cricket, too, and captained the England team to win the first women's World Cup in 1973. She was England captain for a period of twelve years before controversially being left out of the team for the second World Cup in 1977.

The Women's World Cup

The women's cricket World Cup has now been contested five times with Australia having won three and England two.

The growing strength of the women's game was recognized at the last World Cup in 1993 when the final was played at cricket's most famous ground, Lord's in London.

In one-day internationals, she averaged 58.4 runs. In addition to her batting strength, she was also a very effective wicket-keeper and one of her achievements was to hit the first ever six in a women's Test match in 1963.

Like many other top sports people, Heyhoe-Flint also excelled at other sports, in particular at field hockey, at which she played for England as a goalkeeper.

◀ As well as her great skills Rachel Heyhoe-Flint brought a combination of enthusiasm and determination to cricket.

Brian Lara
West Indies/Trinidad & Tobago, born 1969

Brian Lara quite simply is the best batsman playing cricket today. Born in Trinidad and Tobago, Lara first made his mark with an innings of 277 runs against Australia during the West Indies Tour of 1992–3.

However, his greatest moment so far was in the fifth Test against England in 1994. Lara made 375 runs, the highest score ever in a Test match.

In the 1994 English season Lara carried on where he had left off in the West Indies. He scored centuries in his first five innings and then he set a new record in first-class cricket of 501 not out in a match against Durham.

Lara's innings of 501 not out passed numerous landmarks as it was being compiled. The records beaten include: Warwickshire record (previously 305); best score by a West Indian in England (322); best score made this century in England (405); best score ever made in England (424); and best score in first-class cricket (499).

▼ Brian Lara is not a big man but his speed and timing mean that when he is in form the runs are scored very quickly indeed.

Richie Richardson
West Indies/Antigua, born 1962

NEWCASTLE-UNDER-LYME
COLLEGE LIBRARY

Richie Richardson took over as the captain of the West Indies cricket team in 1992. A careful and elegant stroke-player, he has been recognizable for most of his career by his unwillingness to wear a protective helmet when batting. For some years, a sun hat was his trademark, but he has now joined the ranks of cricketers who wear helmets.

Richardson first played for the Leeward Islands in the inter-island competition in 1982. By the end of 1983 he had won a place in the international side for their tour of India.

In his first home Test series, against Australia in 1984, he averaged over eighty runs and hit two splendid

centuries, including one in his home island of Antigua. Richardson did not play regularly for the West Indies team until after his achievements in the tour against England in 1991, when he made six centuries and became the player with the most runs on either side in the Test matches. His strong record as West Indies' captain includes series wins over Pakistan, Australia and England.

Fact File

Test matches: 76 games, 5,445 runs,
    fifteen 100s, highest score 194, average 45.75
First-class games: 12,280 career runs,
    thirty-two 100s, highest score
    194 runs , average 41.91 runs
(Up to March 1995)

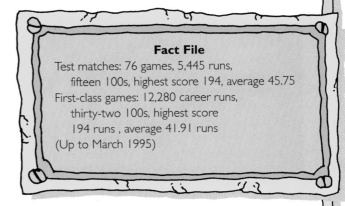
◀ As well as playing in international matches and at home in the West Indies, Richardson played briefly for Yorkshire in the English county championships.

Michael Slater

Australia, born 1970

Michael Slater is one of the brightest stars in world cricket today, and one of the most formidable opening batsmen to come on the scene for a long time.

Slater forced himself into the Australian team in England in 1993 and has never looked back. His best season has been the 1994–5 home season in Australia. He did well against Pakistan, and even better against England. His 176 runs in the first Test is his highest score in international cricket, but he will surely make many more runs for Australia in the years to come.

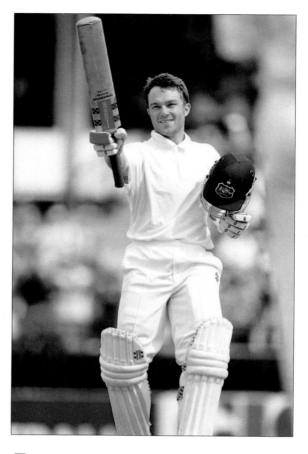

Fact File

Test career: 23 matches, 40 innings
Runs: 2,024 (including six 100s and eight 50s)
Highest score: 176 runs
Average: 51.89 runs
(Up to March 1995)

▼ Michael Slater hits out on the leg side during an Australia-England Test at Adelaide in 1995. Slater went on to make a useful 67 runs in this innings.

Gary Sobers
West Indies/Barbados, born 1936

Gary Sobers was cricket's greatest-ever all rounder. His batting achievements place him close to the top of the all-time averages, and he could bowl almost as well, even more remarkably in any of three different styles.

Born in Barbados, he was first chosen to play for the West Indies team in 1954 as a slow left-arm finger-spin bowler, but he soon blossomed as a batsman. His first Test century in 1957 was his best-ever innings, his score of 365 runs (not out) standing as the record individual Test score for 37 years.

Above all, he did everything with great style and good humour, winning not just the respect but the liking and admiration of opponents and fans everywhere. He was knighted in 1975.

▼ Gary Sobers with one of the many trophies that he and his teams won during his wonderful cricket career.

Malcolm Nash's Embarrassment
On 31 August 1968, Sobers became the first man ever to hit a six off all six balls of an over in a first-class match.
Malcolm Nash of Glamorgan was the unfortunate bowler, and a television crew was present to record the whole thing.

Shane Warne
Australia, born 1969

For the last twenty to thirty years, the real match-winning performances in international cricket have mainly been by fast bowlers. The West Indies, Australia and Pakistan teams have all been able to call upon devastating pace bowlers. The one great exception to this rule has been Shane Warne who, almost single-handedly, has brought the nearly-forgotten art of wrist-spin bowling back into fashion.

Warne has worked hard at his game, developing both his ability to spin the ball sharply and the essential control of line and length to accompany it. He has gradually added new types of delivery to his range of tricks, and has learned how to fool even the best batsmen some of the time.

Warne did not do particularly well in his first Test matches, but in the

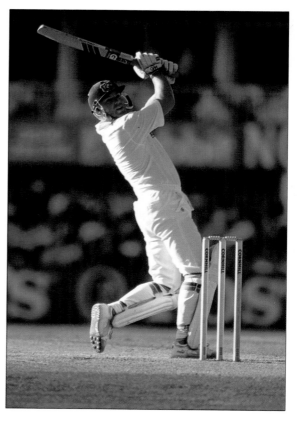

▲ Shane Warne makes some runs of his own.

Warne's first ball in a Test in England has been called the 'ball of the century'. Bowled to the experienced England player Mike Gatting it spun so far and so viciously that Gatting, who had played a textbook defensive shot, did not even touch it. Most players look annoyed or disappointed when they get out. Gatting simply looked bewildered – he had never seen anything like it before.

1992–3 season he produced top-class performances in home matches for Australia against the West Indies and New Zealand. Warne's finest achievements have been in Test series against England both in Australia and in other countries. He took 34 wickets in the series in England in 1993, and 27 wickets at home in 1994–5.

◀ The batsman's problem seems simple, but is very difficult: 'Which way is it going to spin?'

Seve Ballesteros
Spain, born 1957

During the 1980s, the USA's domination of the world of golf was threatened by Europe, and at the head of the challenge was Spain's finest-ever player, Severiano Ballesteros.

Ballesteros has always been exciting to watch. Sometimes his great power and attacking style go wildly wrong. But when this happens he treats the crowd to an exhibition of great recovery shots, playing impossibly delicate chips from the worst of lies and somehow walking away with birdies.

Ballesteros won five major championships during the 1980s (three British Opens and two US Masters), and is still capable of adding to that score.

▼ The full, high follow-through that completes Seve Ballesteros' golf swing shows the power that he puts into his shots.

Golf's most famous team competition is the Ryder Cup, which is held every two years between teams of the best US and European professionals. Ballesteros was the inspiration for the European win in 1985 in Britain, followed by the first-ever European success in the USA in 1987.

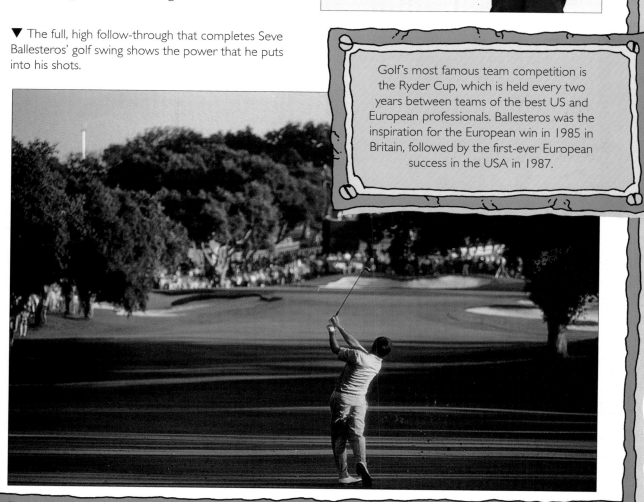

Laura Davies

Great Britain, born 1963

At the moment, Laura Davies is the most formidable woman golfer playing in the world. Her best season to date was in 1994 when she won seven tournaments including the US LPGA, one of four major tournaments in women's professional golf. She also topped both the US money list and the world rankings while still playing in enough tournaments to come third on the European money list.

Davies is a very powerful player, hitting the ball incredible distances. But she matches that skill with a delicacy and sureness of touch on and around the greens where tournaments are so often lost and won.

▲ Laura Davies has a powerful long-distance shot.

▼ Laura Davies at work – absolute concentration on the putting green.

Some golfers practise endlessly to achieve consistency, but Davies spends less time than most practising – an approach that obviously pays off for her. Davies also became the first British player to win one of the major tournaments on the US Tour when she took the 1987 US Open.

In 1994, Davies had eight tournament wins world-wide. In the USA: LPGA and two other tournaments, twelve top-ten finishes, prize money US $687,201, stroke average 70.91 per round. In Europe: two tournament wins in Scotland and Ireland, prize money £59,384 In the rest of the world: tournament wins in Thailand, Japan and Australia.

Nick Faldo
Great Britain, born 1957

Nick Faldo is one of the hardest workers in professional golf. His determined and painstaking search for the perfect swing has been amply rewarded with a host of tournament successes and major championship titles.

No sports person can ever achieve perfection, but in the late 1980s and early 1990s Faldo came nearer than most. He won the British Open in 1987, 1990 and 1992; the US Masters in 1989 and 1990 and added a runner-up and third place spot in each of the British Open, US Open and US PGA.

Faldo is still challenging for honours at the highest level and surely has many more tournament wins to come.

▶ Nick Faldo shows the perfect body position in the fraction of a second after he has played this shot.

▼ Nick Faldo played on the US Tour in 1995 after his many years of success in Europe. He is seen here during the 1995 Phoenix Open.

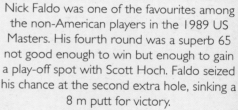

Nick Faldo was one of the favourites among the non-American players in the 1989 US Masters. His fourth round was a superb 65 not good enough to win but enough to gain a play-off spot with Scott Hoch. Faldo seized his chance at the second extra hole, sinking a 8 m putt for victory.

Bobby Jones
USA, 1902–71

Bobby Jones was one the world's greatest-ever golfers. He is the only man to have won a 'grand slam' of the four top tournaments in a single year.

Bobby Jones played his best golf in the 1920s when many of the top players, including himself, were amateurs. From 1923-29 he won eight of what were then golf's biggest championships. But, while he was doing this, he was not even a full-time golfer!

In 1930, he concentrated on his golf and established a record that may well never be matched. He began by winning the British Amateur at St Andrews and then won both the British and US Opens before finishing his Grand Slam in triumph in the US Amateur at Merion in Pennsylvania.

► ▼ Two pictures of Bobby Jones on the way to winning the 1927 British Open, one of his thirteen major championship successes.

Jones and the Masters
Jones' lasting legacy to golf was in establishing the US Masters tournament in 1934, held every year at the beautiful Augusta National Course. The winner of the Masters receives an unusual trophy, a special green jacket, presented each year by the defending champion from the year before.

Nancy Lopez
USA, born 1957

There have been times in the history of women's golf when the skills of its players have not received the attention they deserve. Nowadays, the game is very healthy and much of that success is owed to the influence of Nancy Lopez.

If there has been one thing missing in Lopez's distinguished playing career it has been a win in the US Ladies Open. She has had far more success in another major championship, the Ladies Professional Golfers Association or LPGA, which she won in 1978, 1985 and 1989.

Lopez's great contribution to women's golf was recognized by her election to the Golfing Hall of Fame in 1987, as soon as she was eligible.

The Women's 'Majors'
Like men's professional golf, the women's scene has four tournaments regarded as the most important. These are the US Open, the US LPGA Championship, the Nabisco Dinah Shore, and the du Maurier Classic. No player has yet won a 'grand slam' of all four.

▼ The grass divots fly up but Nancy Lopez's ball has long gone as she fires another approach shot into the heart of the green.

Jack Nicklaus
USA, born 1940

Jack Nicklaus is considered to be the world's best-ever golfer. He took up the game when he was ten years old and scored 51 for his first nine holes. When he was thirteen, he played a round in 69 shots, so it was obvious even then that he was going to be very good.

'Big Jack' and 'the Golden Bear' were Nicklaus' nicknames. He was known for his very long hitting, but his real championship-winning qualities were his fierce concentration and determination to win.

Golf has four major championships – the US Open, the US PGA, the US Masters and the British Open – which are played every year. Since his first success in the 1962 US Open, Nicklaus has won a major professional championship eighteen times, better

than any other player ever. It is a record that will probably never be beaten.

Nicklaus is still winning a lot of money on the US Seniors' Tour and continues to compete in some of the major tournaments on the regular professional circuit.

Fact File
Major Championship Wins: 18 (the most ever)
US Open 1962, 1967, 1972, 1980
US PGA 1963, 1971, 1973, 1975, 1980
US Masters 1963, 1965, 1966, 1972, 1975, 1986
British Open 1966, 1970, 1978
Other Tournaments: US Amateur 1959, 1961
Leading money winner in US PGA tour 8 times

◀ By the look on Big Jack's face this is one putt that did not go in the hole, from the 1980 British Open at Muirfield, won by Tom Watson.

Greg Norman
Australia, born 1955

Greg Norman is Australia's best-ever golfer, and has been one of the sport's biggest stars in the 1980s and 1990s.

Norman has had a great career, winning the British Open twice among sixty-plus tournament wins world-wide. Among all the successes there have been heartbreaks too. Four times Norman has lost in play-offs in the major championships.

Norman is accordingly known by two very different nicknames. To his fans he is known as the 'Great White Shark'. Others call him the 'Great White Flag' for the number of times when he has, they say, given up when he could have won a big tournament. However he is still up at the top of the rankings and still challenging for the big prizes.

▼ Greg Norman won the British Open at Turnberry in 1986. The lighthouse beside the course's 9th tee is one of its best-known landmarks.

Norman's first British Open win was achieved at the Turnberry course in Scotland in 1986 when he alone coped well with difficult windy conditions. In 1993 at St George's in southern England, the fine weather made low scoring easier and Norman produced the Open's lowest ever total score of 267.

Arnold Palmer
USA, born 1929

Arnold Palmer was golf's first superstar. His attacking style brought him a host of adoring fans, 'Arnie's Army', and won him many tournaments with dramatic come-from-behind victories.

Palmer turned professional after winning the 1954 US Amateur Championship. His best win was in the 1960 US Open, played at Cherry Hills in Denver. Palmer was seven shots behind the leader after the third round, but had a round of 65 on the last afternoon to win by two strokes.

Palmer was the first golfer to win over US $1 million in his career. This was a fitting achievement as it was his skill and personality that had made golf into a top international sport.

The End of an Era
Great rivals and friends, Arnold Palmer and Jack Nicklaus both decided that the 1995 British Open would be their last. Fittingly, it was held at St Andrews in Scotland, the home of golf, where both had previously recorded great British Open wins.

▲▼ Arnold Palmer's attacking play meant that he often had to get out of trouble – which he did with style. The pictures above and below were taken at the Masters tournament which he won four times.

Nick Price
Zimbabwe, born 1957

From time to time in every sport a player appears who is universally regarded as the best in the world. In the mid-1990s one modest Zimbabwean emerged as the best golfer in the world.

Nick Price started the 1990s near the top of the world rankings, but not yet a superstar. He had a fine win in the US PGA in 1992. In 1993 he topped the money list on the US Tour, and 1994 was better still. He again led the money winners on the US Tour with five first place finishes, and these included another PGA win.

Earlier in the year he had come to the British Open and produced a brilliant finish to snatch a prize he had come close to gaining twice before.

▼ Nick Price hits his drive at probably the most famous hole in golf, the 18th at the Old Course at St Andrews, the traditional home of the game in Scotland. The historic Royal and Ancient club-house is in the background.

The 1994 Majors
The 1994 season was the first time ever that none of golf's four biggest tournaments was won by an American.
In addition to Price's two wins, South Africa's Ernie Els won the US Open and Spain's José Maria Olazabal won the US Masters.

Nikolai Andrianov
USSR, born 1952

Nikolai Andrianov holds the record number of Olympic medals of any man in any sport. His total of fifteen (seven gold, five silver and three bronze) was achieved in 1972, 1976 and 1980.

Andrianov's best discipline in the range of skills that make up gymnastics competitions was the rings exercise, where he had the special combination of power and seemingly effortless control that marks a true champion. He was twice world champion on the rings in 1974 and 1978, but only won the Olympic gold at this event once in 1976, as compared with his two golds each for the floor exercises and vault.

Andrianov first came to international notice in the 1971 European championships, in which he achieved third place overall. The 1976 Olympics was clearly his best competitive performance. He won the individual all-around title to add to his three other golds in the apparatus sections.

> **Men's Gymnastic Competitions**
> Theoretically it is possible for a male gymnast to win eight medals in a single major competition. Male gymnasts compete in six different exercises, plus the individual and team all-round titles. The six exercises are horizontal bar, parallel bars, vault, pommel horse, rings, and floor exercise.

▶ Nikolai Andrianov on the way to winning the gold medal for the rings exercise at the 1976 Olympic Games in Montreal. He manages to look fairly relaxed despite the great power needed to achieve perfect balance in this position.

Vera Càslàvska
Czechoslovakia, born 1942

Vera Càslàvska was the leading women's gymnast at both the 1964 and 1968 Olympics. She holds second place in the list of all-time women Olympic medal winners with a total of seven golds and four silvers.

Càslàvska's first Olympics was in 1960 when she took a silver medal with the Czech team. She won a gold medal for the vault at the 1962 world championships, and travelled to the 1964 Tokyo Olympics as one of the favourites for the gymnastics competition. She did not disappoint her fans, beating the previous champion, Larissa Latynina, into second place in the competition for the all-round title, and winning two individual golds in the vault and beam.

In the 1968 Olympics, Càslàvska also won three individual golds (in the all-round competition, asymmetric bars and floor). This was especially brave because Czechoslovakia, her home country, had just been invaded by the Soviet Union and Càslàvska was a strong supporter of the government that had been overturned by the communists. She even had to do some of her training while she was in hiding for fear of being arrested.

> Càslàvska shared the gold medal for the floor exercises at the 1968 Mexico Olympics with a Soviet athlete, Larissa Petrik, but there was no doubt who won the hearts of the crowd. Càslàvska chose to perform her routine to the music of the Mexican Hat Dance, which helped to endear her to the fans in Mexico City.

▼ Vera Càslàvska pauses beautifully to show off her grace and balance during a beam exercise competition.

Nadia Comaneci
Romania, born 1961

Standards and records in most sports are usually gradually improved or beaten, but some of Nadia Comaneci's performances can never be bettered because they were judged to be absolutely perfect.

Gymnastics had begun to be made really popular with the charming skills displayed by the Russian gymnast Olga Korbut at the 1972 Olympics, but it was not until Comaneci came to the Montreal Olympics in 1976 that the sport truly took off.

Her flying, tumbling performances on the asymmetric (uneven) parallel bars and on the beam apparatus captured the hearts of the watching world. She was awarded a total of seven perfect scores of ten and came home with three gold medals. She was the first person ever to achieve a perfect score in gymnastics.

▲ After her stunning performance in 1976, Nadia won many other competitions, including two more Olympic gold medals in 1980.

When Comaneci won her first Olympic titles, she was 14 years old, stood 1.49 m tall and weighed 39 kg.
By 1980 she had grown to 1.60 m and weighed 48 kg. It says much for her determination that she was still able to compete and win, despite the changes that had taken place in her physique.

Larissa Latynina
USSR, born 1934

Larissa Latynina was one of the finest-ever gymnasts. She performed at a time when female gymnasts concentrated more on ballet-like grace of movement rather than the tumbling moves that have become fashionable in recent years.

Latynina had originally trained as a ballet dancer and this was most clearly seen in the floor exercises element of her gymnastics routines. She won the floor exercises in each Olympics at which she competed (1956, 1960 and 1964).

In world and Olympic gymnastic competitions, Latynina won more gold medals than any other competitor. Altogether her medals totalled twelve individual and five team golds, as well as nine silvers and five bronzes. Her total of eighteen Olympic medals is also a record for any competitor (man or woman) in any sport.

▲ Larissa Latynina performs her floor exercises routine during the 1960 Olympic Games in Rome. Her performance was good enough to win the gold medal.

◀ In 1964 at Tokyo Latynina starred in the floor exercises and took gold once more.

Fact File
Latynina's Olympic gold medals:
1956: all-around, floor, vault and team
1960: all-around, floor and team
1964: floor and team (silver in the all-around competition)

Montreal Canadiens
Canada, founded 1909

Only two of the teams that were part of the National Hockey League (NHL) when it was formed in 1917 are still playing today, the Toronto Maple Leafs (first known as the Toronto Arenas) and the sport's most successful team ever, the Montreal Canadiens.

The Canadiens first began to delight fans in their hockey-mad city in 1909, when they played in what was then known as the National Hockey Association. In 1917, the team won their first major trophy, the Stanley Cup, in a play-off with the champions of the then operating Pacific Coast Hockey Association.

Since the formation of the NHL, the Canadiens have put their name on its top trophy another twenty-three times,

almost twice as many times as their closest rivals. Their greatest years were from the mid-1950s through the 1970s, when they won the championship an amazing fifteen times.

The Canadiens' great players have included the brilliant but volatile Maurice 'Rocket' Richard and, throughout the 1970s successes, the speedy sharpshooter Guy La Fleur.

The Canadiens' first sight of glory after they joined the NHL came in the Stanley Cup finals in 1919, but this ended disappointingly when, with the series tied, it had to be abandoned because of a flu epidemic. This is the only time since it was established in 1893 that the Stanley Cup has not been won.

▼ The Canadiens' familiar red uniforms lead the chase for the puck in this 1992 game with the Chicago Blackhawks.

Wayne Gretzky
Canada, born 1961

Wayne Gretzky is known simply to ice hockey fans as 'The Great One'. Gretzky first made his mark in the 1979–80 season when he became the youngest player ever to be top scorer in the NHL. From then until the present, the records have continued to be broken – more than sixty at the last count.

In the 1980s, he won at least one of the game's top individual trophies every year, and from 1980 to 1985 he won and retained both the Hart Trophy as the league's MVP and the Ross Trophy as top points scorer.

The crowning moment came in March 1994 when he scored his 802nd goal, passing Gordie Howe's long-standing NHL record.

▶▼ Both pictures show Wayne Gretzky in action with the Los Angeles Kings whom he joined in 1988. As a professional he first played briefly for the Indianapolis Racers and from 1979-88 for the Edmonton Oilers.

Despite all his scoring records, Gretzky does not think of himself as a particularly great goal scorer. Nor does he have unique power or pace on the ice. Instead, Gretzky would prefer to be remembered for his play-making skills and ability to read the game which, to most fans, are simply the best ever.

Gordie Howe
Canada, born 1928

Professional ice hockey is a fast, furious and tough sport, and no place for anyone who cannot look after themselves. One man is a legend for setting records in five decades with an active professional career of thirty-two years and over 2,000 games.

Gordie Howe joined the Detroit Red Wings in the US National Hockey League (NHL) in 1946 when he was aged nineteen, and he did not finally hang up his skates and retire for good until 1980 when he left the Hartford Whalers at the age of fifty-one.

Howe was a big man, 1.93 m tall and weighing 93 kg, but he matched his size with speed around the ice and very impressive hockey stick handling skills.

Most of the NHL records he set have since been overtaken by the astonishing Wayne Gretzky. However, if his 1970s career in the World Hockey Association is included, Howe is still far ahead with 2,358 career points, including 975 goals.

All in the Family

It is quite common for brothers or sisters to play together at the highest levels of sport. However, when Howe made his come-back with Houston in 1973, he achieved a rather different distinction, joining his sons Marty and Mark in the team.

▼ The hair may have been grey (or at least what was left of it) but Gordie Howe was still quick enough to win the puck and score in this game in his last season.

Sven Tumba
Sweden, born 1931

The Swedes, like the Canadians, are crazy about ice hockey and Sven Tumba was one of their greatest-ever stars.

He also represented his country in soccer (in five internationals) and golf, even though he only took up playing golf seriously after his long ice hockey career was over. He played for Sweden in golf's 1974 World Cup.

As an ice hockey player, he led the Swedish team for most of the 1950s and 1960s. He won Olympic medals with the team in 1952 and 1964. Sweden also won the World Championship in 1953, 1957 and 1962.

▶ Tumba (centre) at the World Championships at Tammerfors in 1965.

▼ Tumba celebrates a goal against Canada during the 1965 World Championships.

The oddest thing about Sven Tumba was that his real name was Sven Johansson. He became so famous that he started to be called Tumba instead, after the suburb of Stockholm where he lived as a child.

Bonnie Blair
USA, born 1964

The attention of most ice skating fans at the 1994 Winter Olympics was concentrated on the headline-grabbing quarrel between USA's Tonya Harding and Nancy Kerrigan. However, while all that was going on, Bonnie Blair earned a place in the record books for her performances on the ice, not her activities off it.

Blair first won a place in the US Olympic speed skating team in 1984, but did not figure in the medals in those games. In 1986, she set her first-ever world record over 500 metres on the 111-metres 'short track', and followed this up with a 500-metres 'long track' record the next year (the 'long' or standard track is 400 metres to a lap).

Blair's first Olympic win came in the 500 metres in the 1988 Games, and the time she set in her gold-medal performance, after an especially quick

America's Finest – Blair or Heiden?
Before Blair, America's best-ever speed skater was unquestionably Eric Heiden. Both have won five Olympic golds, but on a strict medal count Blair comes out on top because of the single bronze medal she gained in 1988.

start, remains the Olympic record. She also won bronze in the 1,000 metre race.

At the 1992 and 1994 Winter Olympics, she was at the top of her form winning both the sprints in both games. Blair has also won other important competitions including the 1994 World Cup at both her distances.

◀ Bonnie Blair in training in 1991 showing all the concentration and determination that have made her such a great champion.

Irina Rodnina
USSR, born 1949

Irina Rodnina has the greatest-ever competitive record of any figure skater. Her event was the pairs skating and she recorded her record number of medal-winning performances amazingly with two different partners, first Aleksei Ulanov and then Aleksandr Zaitsev.

Rodnina won ten successive World Championships from 1969 to 1978. For the first four she was with Ulanov and the remainder with Zaitsev.

Rodnina and Ulanov also won the gold medal at the 1972 Olympics, but then she began competing with Zaitsev, whom she married in 1976.

Rodnina remained undefeated in the European, World and Olympic championships with Zaitsev from 1973 to 1978, and added a third Olympic title to her list in 1980. She only missed out in 1979 because she took time off to have their baby.

▲ In pairs skating the competitors must have strength and timing for the lifts and jumps.

▼ And grace and elegance for the dance sections.

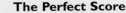

The Perfect Score
Zaitsev was probably the better partner for Rodnina, on the ice as well as off it, for it was with him at the 1973 European Championships that they achieved a completely perfect score, gaining marks of six from all twelve judges.

Torvill & Dean
Great Britain

Jayne Torvill and Christopher Dean have been perhaps the finest ever exponents of the graceful and stylish art of ice dancing. They came fifth in the 1980 Olympics and then their great days really began. They won four successive World Championships from 1981 to 1984, each time producing superbly arranged and beautifully executed new routines in the original and free dance sections.

Their Barnum routine won them nine maximum six scores for artistic interpretation at the 1983 World Championships. However, their finest routine of all was undoubtedly their stunning interpretation of Ravel's *Bolero*, which they produced for the 1984 Olympics and World Championships, both of which they won.

In the World Championships, they received thirteen maximum marks out of a possible eighteen, the best ice dance performance ever.

They then turned professional and toured very successfully with their own ice show, but were allowed to return to international competition in the 1994 Olympics. Their 1994 season started well when they won the European Championship. Then, sadly, the dream of Olympic gold went wrong when part of their routine was judged to include illegal moves. The marks lost meant they had to settle for the bronze medal.

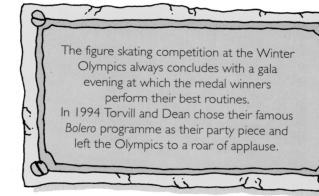

The figure skating competition at the Winter Olympics always concludes with a gala evening at which the medal winners perform their best routines.
In 1994 Torvill and Dean chose their famous *Bolero* programme as their party piece and left the Olympics to a roar of applause.

◀ In training for the 1994 Olympics. Fans may have thought that Torvill and Dean were as good as ever but the judges disagreed.

Mal Meninga
Australia, born 1960

Big Mal Meninga was one of the most powerful and effective runners ever to play rugby league. A superb centre, he matched his own ball-carrying abilities with the passing skills to make scoring opportunities for his team-mates. He rounded all this off with accurate goal kicking that gave him point-scoring records.

Meninga first played for the Australian team against New Zealand in July 1982. Later that year they toured Britain undefeated in fifteen matches.

Even among the brilliance of that special team, Meninga was top scorer with 118 points, including six tries from his ten appearances.

The Australians were almost as impressive again during their 1986 UK tour, undefeated in thirteen matches with Meninga appearing in eleven of them and scoring five tries this time. Meninga also played for the Australians in many of the matches in the 1988 World Cup, but missed the final because of injury.

He was appointed captain of Australia in 1990 for the next UK tour. Their loss in the first Test was the first time the Australians had lost in the UK since 1978. However, Meninga scored a try in that game and in both of the winning performances that completed the series.

State of Origin
Some of the world's finest rugby league is played in Australia's State of Origin matches between all-star teams from Queensland and New South Wales. Meninga is a Queenslander and was captain of the Queensland team in the later part of his career.

◀ Big Mal Meninga was an effective goal kicker as well as being a powerful runner. As the picture shows he used the old fashioned 'straight ahead' style of kicking.

Michael Lynagh
Australia, born 1963

Michael Lynagh is the all-time record points scorer in international rugby union. In his international career from 1984 to 1995 he became the first and only player to score more than 900 points in international matches.

He played his first match for Australia against Fiji in 1984, and scored in that and almost every other match he played for his country. Most of his points came from deadly goal kicking, but he also scored many useful tries.

Lynagh's tactical leadership and handling skills were one of the key elements in the success of the Australian team. The high point for Lynagh and his team-mates came in the 1991 World Cup which they won by beating England in the final.

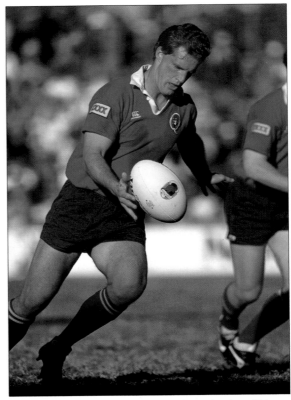

▲ In his native Australia Michael Lynagh played his senior rugby with Queensland and is seen here wearing their colours in 1991.

▼ Lynagh sets up an Australian attack during a game against England.

One of Lynagh's best and most important Australian tries was scored against Ireland in the 1991 World Cup. Ireland went ahead in the final minutes of the game but, with defeat and elimination looming, the Australians did not panic. Lynagh began a brilliant handling move that he himself finished off by diving over to score a try in the corner.

Gavin Hastings
Great Britain/Scotland, born 1962

Gavin Hastings was a powerful full back for the Scotland rugby team and an impressive captain of his own country and the British Isles team.

Gavin Hastings made his first appearance for Scotland in 1986 and from then until his retirement in 1995 was regarded as one of the strongest running and tackling full backs in world rugby.

Hastings's total of 667 points in his sixty games for Scotland, plus 63 points in internationals with the British Lions, places him very close to the top of the all-time points scoring table.

Hastings was a member of Scotland's Grand Slam winning team in the Five Nations championship in 1990, and later in his career his captaincy of Scotland, and of the British Lions on their tour of New Zealand in 1993, was much praised for his leadership on and off the field. He brought his career to an end with record scoring performances in the 1995 World Cup.

A Short-Lived Record

Gavin Hastings scored a Scottish individual record of 44 points against World Cup outsiders, the Ivory Coast, in 1995. This was a world record at the time, but it only lasted a couple of days until New Zealand comprehensively demolished Japan in another World Cup game.

▼ ▶ Gavin Hastings in the blue of Scotland (below) against Fiji in 1989, and in British Lions red (above) in 1993.

Will Carling
Great Britain/England, born 1965

Will Carling has been the most successful captain ever of the England rugby union team. He is a strong running and tackling centre, and has scored spectacular tries in many important matches.

Before Carling's captaincy, England had many very good players, but seldom combined their talents to create a successful team. Since Carling became captain, they have won three Grand Slams in the Five Nations championship, in 1991, 1992 and 1995.

These results brought England into both the 1991 and 1995 World Cups as one of the best teams. Carling and his men had the disappointment of losing in the final in 1991 to Australia, and in the semi-final in 1995 to New Zealand. But without Carling they would probably never have got as far in either tournament.

▶ Will Carling in action for the Barbarians all-star invitation team.

▼ Carling, ball in hand, leads an England attack against Australia.

Off the field, Carling has used his captaincy experience to teach business people the skills of working together as a team, and how to make the best use of each others' talents. Managers in many types of office work have learned lessons that Carling discovered among the mud and sweat of the rugby field.

Gareth Edwards
Great Britain/Wales, born 1947

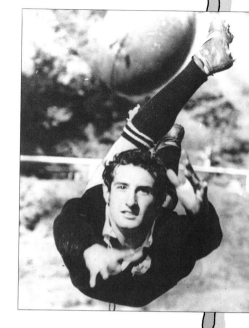

Many people believe that Gareth Edwards was the finest scrum-half ever to play rugby union. Edwards first played international rugby for his home country of Wales in 1967 when he was only nineteen years old. From then until his retirement in 1978, he was never dropped and never missed an international because of injury. He eventually won 53 caps – a record at the time.

In addition to his appearances for Wales, he was also selected for three British Isles touring sides and played in ten tests. His tours included the most successful ever to New Zealand in 1971 and to South Africa in 1974, in both of which he was one of the key members of the team.

He was always a threatening runner, particularly strong and skilled at breaking opposition defences for vital close range scores. His total of twenty international tries is far and away the best ever achieved by a scrum half.

▼ Gareth Edwards in action for the British Isles. The British Isles team, known as the British Lions, never plays in Britain but only in matches in other countries.

During his career, Edwards was fortunate to play with two of the finest-ever outside halves who have played for both Wales and the Lions. Barry John was his team mate in the Cardiff club as well as with Wales and the Lions in 1971.
John retired in 1974, but Phil Bennett was his equally effective replacement.

Bjørn Dæhlie
Norway, born 1967

Bjørn Dæhlie is joint top of the Winter Olympics all-time gold medal winning table, and his three silvers in addition to his five golds place him second on the list of winners of all types of medal.

Dæhlie has been a star at the last two Winter Olympic Games in 1992 and 1994. At the 1992 Olympics, Dæhlie won his first three golds in the 15-km freestyle pursuit, 50-km classical and in the relay with the Norwegian team.

In 1994, he again won four medals, this time two golds and two silvers. The relay race in which Dæhlie was second was probably the most dramatic event of the whole 1994 games.

▲ Bjørn Dæhlie strides out to win one of his great collection of medals at the 1994 Winter Olympics.

▼ Here he overtakes a competitor with an earlier start time to win gold in the 10 km cross country.

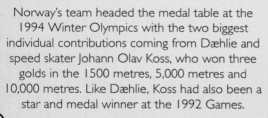

Norway's team headed the medal table at the 1994 Winter Olympics with the two biggest individual contributions coming from Dæhlie and speed skater Johann Olav Koss, who won three golds in the 1500 metres, 5,000 metres and 10,000 metres. Like Dæhlie, Koss had also been a star and medal winner at the 1992 Games.

Annemarie Moser-Pröll
Austria, born 1953

Annemarie Moser-Pröll of Austria was one of the finest-ever women's downhill and giant slalom skiers. She holds the women's record total of sixty-two wins in World Cup races.

As Annemarie Pröll (until her marriage in 1975), she became the youngest-ever overall World Cup champion in 1971, and dominated the sport for the rest of the 1970s (apart from 1976 when she did not compete).

Moser-Pröll was overall World Cup champion six times (in 1971–75 and in 1979). In her 'poor' years of 1977, 1978 and 1980 she was second.

Moser-Pröll won two silver medals in the 1972 Olympics and did not compete in 1976. In 1980 it seemed that she might miss out on the top medals once again but on the day Moser-Pröll avenged earlier defeats and took the downhill gold.

▲ Annemarie Moser-Pröll (right) and one of her Austrian team-mates during the 1974 season.

NEWCASTLE-UNDER-LYME
COLLEGE LIBRARY

The Alpine Combined Events
The downhill skiing races are a test of the skiers' speed, while the various types of slalom race put more emphasis on weaving and turning. The overall or Alpine Combined title combines the points achieved in these very different skills – Annemarie Moser-Pröll won it in six World Cups.

◄ Annemarie Moser-Pröll's strongest event was downhill racing in which she was World Cup champion seven times.

Alberto Tomba

Italy, born 1966

Italian winter sports fans had one big favourite in the late 1980s and early 1990s, Alberto Tomba, who is one of the finest-ever slalom skiers.

Tomba has reserved his top performances for the Olympic Games seasons – 1987–8 was his best year. He was World Cup winner in both the slalom and giant slalom for his performances throughout the season, and he won gold medals in the 1988 Olympics in both events.

The next Olympic year of 1992 was almost as good. Again he won the World Cup in both of his events, but this time he had to settle for a single Olympic gold in the giant slalom. He was back again at the Winter Olympics in 1994, winning a silver medal in the slalom

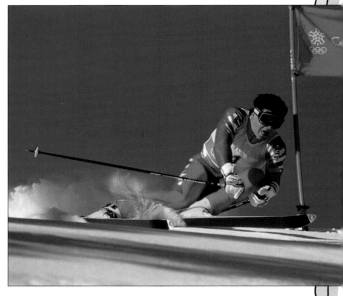

▲ Tomba on his way to the slalom gold at the 1988 Calgary Olympics.

races to round off a season when he took the overall slalom title.

Because Tomba does not race in the downhill, it is impossible for him to win the Alpine Combined title. However, he has had so many slalom wins that he has three times been second and twice third in the Combined competition.

▼ Tomba prepares for a race in 1993.

Tomba's wealthy father had promised to buy him a Ferrari sports car if he won an Olympic gold medal. Half way through the giant slalom competition in 1988, Alberto was so confident that he could hang on to his first-round lead that he found a phone and called his father, just to remind him of his promise. He duly won his car.

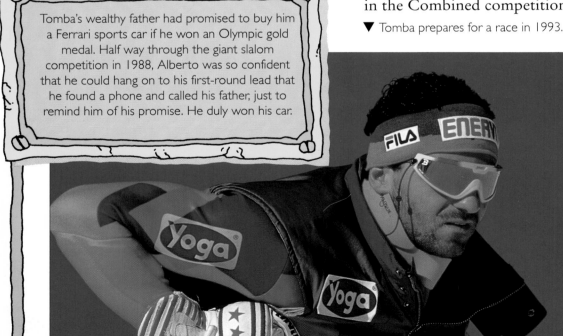

Matti Nykänen
Finland, born 1963

Ski jumping is a sport in which the top stars must combine aggression and strength with poise and control. If they manage to achieve this, they will get the best possible lift off from the ski ramp and fly efficiently through the air. Matti Nykänen was simply the best at this difficult combination for most of the 1980s.

Matti Nykänen demonstrated his superiority most convincingly in the Olympic Games. On the 70-metre hill, he won silver in 1984, and gold in 1988.

His jumping on the large 90-metre hill was even better. He took the gold medal in both 1984 and 1988, and was part of the winning Finnish team on the 90-metre hill in 1988 when this was first made a team event.

▼ Matti Nykänen's first round jump in winning the 1988 Olympic 90-metre gold medal was 118.5 metres, the longest ever in an Olympics.

Eddie the Eagle
While Nykänen was winning his gold medals in 1988, a British competitor, Eddie 'The Eagle' Edwards, was entertaining the crowds with his bravery, if not with his ski jumping skills. Eddie was last in the competition with less than half of the points scored by the second worst jumper.

Ajax Amsterdam
Netherlands, founded 1900

Ajax of Amsterdam has been one of the best clubs in the Netherlands for many years, but from the 1960s they became one of the best in Europe as well.

Inspired by players such as Johan Cruyff and using the new tactics of 'total football', Ajax won successive European Cups in 1971-73.

Another glory period began in 1987 when they won the Cup Winners Cup. In 1992, Ajax became only the second club to win all three European club competitions when they took the UEFA Cup. Perhaps the sweetest success was still to come, however. In 1995 they again won the European Cup, beating AC Milan in the final.

Total Football

The Ajax team and the Dutch national side in the early 1970s based their tactics around what came to be known as 'total football'. Although players did still specialize in attacking, midfield or defensive play, they were encouraged to take up attacking opportunities whatever position they played on the team.

▼ When Ajax (in dark kit) beat AC Milan 1-0 in the 1995 European Cup Final it was a long delayed revenge. AC Milan had beaten Ajax 4-1 in Ajax's first ever European final in 1970.

Roberto Baggio
Italy, born 1967

Roberto Baggio came to the 1994 World Cup finals with the hopes of the whole of Italy riding on his goal-scoring abilities. Italy scraped through the group stages of the tournament but, when it came to the knock-out games, Baggio seemed ready to be his team's star.

Baggio scored both the Italian goals to put Nigeria out, scored the winner against Spain in the quarter-finals, and both of Italy's two goals against Bulgaria in the semi-finals to gain them a place in the final with Brazil. After all that who could have believed it when Baggio missed the last penalty in the shoot-out to decide the drawn match?

Baggio has played all his club soccer in Italy's famous Serie A league. His first club was Fiorentina and his fans were so disappointed when he left to join Juventus in 1990 that there were riots in the town. Even with Baggio, Juventus found the Italian league title beyond

▲ Baggio playing for Italy in the 1994 World Cup.

Penalty Shoot-outs
The 1994 final was the first time that a World Cup had been won on penalties when the game had been drawn after extra time, although two earlier matches in the 1994 tournament had also gone this way. Three previous World Cup Finals had been won in extra time.

their grasp, but they did win the UEFA Cup in 1993 with Baggio at the top of his form.

That season he was made World and European Player of the Year, but the disappointment of the 1994 World Cup was still to come. Baggio is still one of the game's biggest stars and will have other opportunities to add to his goal-scoring feats.

◀ Roberto Baggio in the famous striped colours of Juventus in an Italian league match.

Franz Beckenbauer
West Germany, born 1945

In his playing career, Franz Beckenbauer won a record total of 103 international caps (since beaten) for West Germany, and captained their winning World Cup side in 1974 when they beat tournament favourites Holland in a closely-contested final.

In club soccer, he played for most of his career with Bayern Munich, winning numerous trophies in the German football league and leading the club to successive European Cup victories in 1974–6.

Beckenbauer led his teams from the heart of the defence. His marking and tackling were excellent, but he is remembered most for his ability to turn defence into attack with decisive passing or his own forward runs, and powerful long-distance shooting.

Later in his career, in 1977, Beckenbauer joined an American team, the New York Cosmos, where he played an important

Fact File
International career: 103 appearances for West Germany
As player: World Cup winners 1974 (as captain), runners-up 1966, semi-finals 1970; European Champions 1972;
As manager: World Cup winners 1990, runners-up 1986
With Bayern Munich: numerous German trophies; European Cup 1974, 1975, 1976

part in the development of soccer in North America.

After he had retired as a player, Beckenbauer had an equally distinguished career as a coach of the West German national team. He managed them to the runners-up spot in the 1986 World Cup, and went one better in Rome four years later when West Germany beat Argentina 1–0 in the final. Beckenbauer is the only man to have both captained and managed a winning World Cup team.

◀ Franz Beckenbauer in action for West Germany against Brazil in 1973. The next year Beckenbauer led his country to a World Cup triumph.

George Best
Great Britain/Northern Ireland, born 1946

George Best was another of the wayward geniuses who seem to be all too common at the highest levels of international soccer.

Throughout his best years Best played with Manchester United and was an undoubted star in English and European club soccer. He could play as a winger or as a central attacker and used his effortless ball control and pace to tease and bewilder his opponents.

1967 brought the finest moment of his career. United reached the European Cup final against Benfica of Portugal, and an outstanding performance by Best helped them to win 4–1 after extra time.

Later in his career he played less successfully in the USA and Scotland as well as for other teams in England.

▼ George Best in the familiar red of Manchester United for whom he played all his finest games.

The Playboy Footballer
George Best was one of the first footballers to live and be treated by fans like a pop star. He dressed in the latest fashions, was seen with beautiful women, and enjoyed going to the top night spots. Unfortunately, this led to his decline as a player, because he also drank too much alcohol and neglected his physical fitness.

Bobby Charlton
Great Britain/England, born 1937

Bobby Charlton was one of the heroes of England's dramatic extra-time win over West Germany in the 1966 World Cup Final, and was selected as European Footballer of the Year in 1966. Charlton made a total of 106 appearances for England (since beaten by two other players) and scored forty-nine goals for his country, which remains the record.

Charlton played for the Manchester United club for almost the whole of his career – in 606 matches he scored 198 goals. Although his powerful shooting and goal-scoring feats are well remembered, Charlton was not an out-and-out striker. His all-round skills made him a brilliant playmaker also.

Since he retired from playing, Charlton has become one of the best-liked and best-known ambassadors of his sport.

▶ Bobby Charlton with the ball in his last game for Manchester United.

▼ A young Charlton shows the power of his shooting.

The Munich Air Disaster
Charlton was one of a group of young players who helped Manchester United to the English championship in 1956 and 1957, and who seemed set to dominate the English game for some years to come. Instead, eight were tragically killed in an air crash when travelling home from a European Cup match in 1958.

Johan Cruyff
Netherlands, born 1947

Johan Cruyff was the leading Dutch soccer player for most of the 1970s. He helped to make the Netherlands one of the most powerful soccer countries in the world.

Cruyff played for Ajax Amsterdam from the start of his career in 1964 until 1973 and later with Barcelona. In his time at Ajax the highlights were when they won the European Cup three years in succession from 1971 to 1973. Cruyff played forty-eight times for the Dutch national team from 1966, including winning a runners-up medal in the 1974 World Cup.

Cruyff had further success as a coach after his retirement, taking Ajax to the European Cup Winners Cup in 1987, and Barcelona to the Cup Winners Cup in 1989 and the European Cup in 1992.

▼ Cruyff often looked ungainly on the football field, until you saw what he could do with the ball.

Cruyff got his start at Ajax thanks to his mother. She worked as a cleaner in the club offices and persuaded them that her young son had the sort of talent that the club needed. They took a look at 12-year-old Johan and quickly signed him up for their youth team. The rest, as they say, is history.

Eusébio
Mozambique/Portugal, born 1942

Eusébio was sometimes described as the 'European Pelé' which was unfair to his own special footballing skills – the most impressive part of his game was his thunderously powerful shooting.

He was born Eusébio Ferreira da Silva in what was then Portuguese East Africa (now Mozambique) but moved to the Benfica club in Portugal in 1961. At this time he became known only by the single name, Eusébio.

Benfica were the best team in Portugal throughout the 1960s and won the European Cup in 1961 and 1962. Eusébio scored two goals in the spectacular 5–3 win in the 1962 final against the Spanish team Real Madrid.

Eusébio played sixty-four games for Portugal and scored forty-one goals. He was top scorer in the 1966 World Cup.

▼ ▶ Two pictures of Eusébio during the 1963 European Cup final. Eusébio scored, but Benfica finally lost 2-1 to AC Milan.

When Eusébio began playing, the top Portuguese clubs recruited the best players from their country's African colonies. SC Lourenco Marques usually sent players to Sporting Lisbon, but when Eusébio came from them to Portugal in 1961, Benfica persuaded him to join them instead.

Inter Milan
Italy, founded 1908

Milan is soccer-mad and Internazionale, as the side is correctly known, is one of the two teams which divides the city's loyalties. Internazionale was founded after a dispute within AC Milan, when a group of supporters set up their own club in protest at AC Milan's owners.

Internazionale soon became one of Italy's most successful clubs and were one of the pioneers of European club competition in the 1930s. In the 1960s, under coach Helenio Herrera, their defensive catenaccio (curtain) formation may not have made for entertaining games, but it was brutally effective.

Internazionale won the European and World Club Championships in 1964 and 1965 and lost in the final in 1967 as their success slipped away. Renewed success came in 1989 with the Italian title, and two UEFA Cup wins in the 1990s.

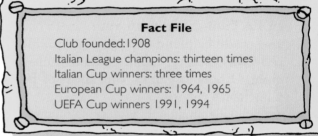

Fact File

Club founded: 1908
Italian League champions: thirteen times
Italian Cup winners: three times
European Cup winners: 1964, 1965
UEFA Cup winners 1991, 1994

Gary Lineker
Great Britain/England, born 1960

Gary Lineker was England's leading goal scorer in the 1980s and one of his country's top marksmen ever. He began his professional career with the modest Leicester City club in 1978, and played with them until 1985 when he joined Everton.

He was English player of the year in 1986, and rounded off a fine season by being overall top scorer in the 1986 World Cup, although England lost in the quarter-finals. Lineker then faced a new challenge with the Spanish club Barcelona, enjoying success when they won the European Cup Winners Cup in 1989.

He returned to England that year to play with Tottenham Hotspur, winning an FA Cup medal with Spurs in 1991 and was made England captain in 1990. He retired with forty-eight goals from his eighty England games, one short of Bobby Charlton's record.

▲ Gary Lineker playing for England (in white) against Scotland (in blue).

Throughout his playing career, Lineker was one of the fairest-ever top players. He was never given a yellow (warning) or red (send off) card for indiscipline by a referee, and this remarkable record was recognized by a special award from soccer's world governing body FIFA.

▼ Gary Lineker playing for England (in white shirts). against Ireland (in green).

Manchester United

Great Britain, founded 1878

Manchester United are not England's most successful team (Liverpool have won twice as many championships), but they are the most famous club and have the most fans both in England and around the world.

Their great days began in 1945 when Matt Busby arrived as manager. The achievements of his best team, the 'Busby Babes', were cruelly cut short when eight of them were killed in an air crash in 1958. One of the survivors was Bobby Charlton, who was joined by Denis Law and George Best in the next great United side of the 1960s.

Recent years have also been very successful. The best result of all was an historic League and Cup double in 1994 which finished with a 4–0 win over Chelsea in the FA Cup Final.

▲ Cantona scores in the 1994 Cup Final win.

Fact File

English League Champions: 1908, 1911, 1952, 1956, 1957, 1965, 1967, 1993, 1994
FA Cup winners: 1909, 1948, 1963, 1977, 1983, 1985, 1990, 1994
European Cup winners: 1968
European Cup Winners Cup winners: 1991
European Supercup winners: 1991

▼ United players celebrate their League win in 1994.

Diego Maradona
Argentina, born 1960

Diego Maradona was the best soccer player in the world from the late 1970s and throughout most of the 1980s. Despite his marvellous skills, his behaviour on and off the field was often unacceptable, and his international career finally ended in disgrace when he was found to have taken drugs to help him to lose weight during the 1994 World Cup.

The first years of his career were spent in his native Argentina, playing mostly for the Argentinos Júniors club. He made his international debut for Argentina at the age of sixteen in 1977. He transferred to Barcelona in Spain in 1982, and moved on from there to Napoli in Italy in 1986, each time for record transfer fees.

Maradona did not play in the Argentina team that won the World Cup in 1978, but was soon a fixture in the side and became its inspiration. His ball

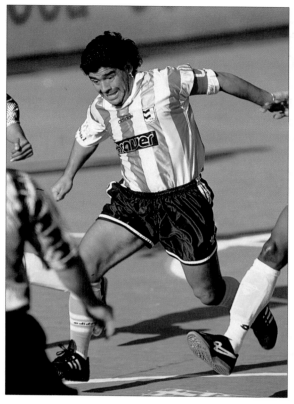

▲ Maradona wearing Argentina colours in a five-a-side match.

control and ability to beat an opponent and make scoring chances out of the slightest opportunity made him a player feared and respected around the world.

He was the mainstay of the Argentina side that won the World Cup in 1986 but, with less able team-mates, had to settle for a runners-up spot in 1990.

Argentina in the World Cup
Argentina rank fourth in the all-time table of results in the World Cup. They were second in the first-ever tournament in 1930, won in 1978 and 1986, and gained second place in 1990. Maradona won the award as the tournament's best player in 1986.

◀ Diego Maradona during his comeback before the 1994 World Cup, when he played for Seville.

Stanley Matthews
Great Britain/England, born 1915

The teams Stanley Matthews played in won only one major trophy, but he is still regarded as one of the greatest players ever to play the game. Matthews was a right winger using his brilliant dribbling skills, deceptive swerve and killing acceleration to leave defenders floundering behind him. Once in the open, he delivered inch-perfect crosses to give his attacking team-mates perfect scoring opportunities.

Matthews first played for Stoke City in 1932 and England in 1934. He was still in the England team twenty-three years later in 1957, and played his last big match in 1965 when he was over 50 years of age.

Matthews won fifty-four international caps with England (eighty-four counting games played during the Second World War), but his only trophy in his club career was an FA Cup winners medal playing for Blackpool in 1953.

▶ Stanley Matthews in the striped shirt of Stoke City which was his first and, much later, his last club.

▼ Matthews (in white) and a Scotland defender in a match in 1944.

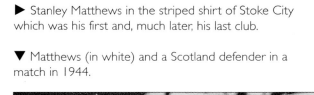

Matthews' Cup Final
The FA Cup Final is English soccer's greatest day. Until near the end of the 1953 final, it seemed that Matthews, twice before on the losing side, would never win that great trophy. His Blackpool team were 3–1 down when Matthews began to find his touch. Bolton's defence was destroyed and Blackpool won 4–3.

Pelé

Brazil, born 1940

Pelé was born Edson Arantes do Nascimento, but under the name by which he is usually known he became the world's best-ever soccer player.

In 1957, aged only seventeen, Pelé scored a goal in the first game he played for Brazil, and in 1958 he was the star of the Brazilian team that won the World Cup. He triumphed again in 1970 in the magnificent Brazil team that won the World Cup, scoring the first goal in the 4–1 win over Italy in the final.

In club soccer, he played for most of his career with Santos, helping them to two South American club championships in the Copa Libertadores in 1962 and 1963, plus many other domestic Brazilian trophies. He played out the final years of his career with the New York Cosmos, helping to increase the popularity of soccer in the USA.

▲ Pelé with his foot beside the ball ready to take a free kick in his last Brazil international in 1971.

Pelé published his life story under the title *My Life and the Beautiful Game*. Most people who saw him remember how he made soccer just that, blending his sparkling skills with his delight in attacking tactics. Many people think that the Brazilian team Pelé starred in in 1970 was the finest ever.

▼ Pelé early in his international career.

Ferenc Puskas
Hungary/Spain, born 1927

Even his own fans said that Ferenc Puskas was unfit and overweight, and that his right foot was only good for standing on, but that was not important since he could do anything he wanted with his left.

Puskas first played for the Kispest club in his native Hungary from 1943, staying with them when they became Honved in 1948. Through the 1950s, Puskas played 84 games for Hungary and scored 83 goals. Unfortunately, he had to settle for a second place medal in the 1954 World Cup.

In 1958, Puskas joined Real Madrid. The Spanish team were the best club side in the world at the time, and Puskas's partnership in attack with the Argentinian Alfredo di Stefano took them to still more honours. They won the European Cup in 1959 and 1960 and the Spanish championship each year between 1961 and 1965.

▶ Puskas (dark shirt) and a Swedish player tussle for the ball in a 1955 game when Puskas was playing for Hungary.

▼ Puskas warms up before a match for Spain against England in 1963.

Puskas's Greatest Game
The European Cup Final in 1960 saw Puskas at his best. His partner Alfredo di Stefano scored three goals, but Puskas scored four as Real Madrid overwhelmed the German team Eintracht Frankfurt 7–3 in what many fans say was the best game they have ever seen.

Michel Platini
France, born 1955

Michel Platini was France's best-ever soccer player, and is the only man ever to win the European Player of the Year award three times in a row (1983–5).

Platini was a gifted midfield organizer. His passing skills opened up opposition defences, and he scored many important goals from free kicks and penalties as well as in open play.

Platini came to the fore with the French club Nancy, which he joined in 1972. He won a place in the French national team in 1976, and eventually won seventy-two caps. He played successfully from 1979 to 1982 with St Etienne in France and from 1982 to 1987 with Juventus in Italy. After he retired in 1987, Platini became coach of the French national team, but was replaced in 1992 after disappointing results.

▲ Platini celebrates a goal for France, World Cup 1986.

The 1998 World Cup
The 1998 World Cup will be held in France with the number of teams competing in the final stages increased to thirty-two. Platini is one of the leaders of the French team that is organizing the tournament.

▼ Platini sets up a shooting opportunity for Juventus.

Marco van Basten
Netherlands, born 1964

Marco van Basten was one of the finest players in the seemingly endless stream of great soccer stars that the Netherlands has produced since the 1960s.

Van Basten's club soccer career began with the famous Ajax club of Amsterdam. His goal-scoring ability helped Ajax to six major trophies in Dutch football and the Cup Winners Cup in 1987.

Later in 1987, van Basten was transferred to AC Milan of Italy. Van Basten was one of the driving forces of the success that followed. Milan won the Italian championship in 1988 and 1993, and took the European Cup in 1989 (with two goals in the final from van Basten) and 1990. He retired in the summer of 1995.

▲ Marco van Basten in Italian league action with AC Milan. Van Basten was European player of the year in 1988, 1989 and 1992.

▼ Van Basten (in orange) was a star with the Dutch national team. He scored in the final when Holland won the European Championship in 1988.

FIFA World Footballer of the Year
This award was officially made for the first time in 1991 and amazingly the first three winners all played in Italy. Lothar Matthäus of Inter Milan and Germany won in 1991, Marco van Basten of AC Milan and the Netherlands in 1992, and Roberto Baggio of Juventus and Italy in 1993.

Taiho
Japan, born 1940

Wrestlers in Japan's national sport of sumo are given special names. Taiho means 'Big Bird' in Japanese, and the man who used this name is regarded as the greatest-ever sumo wrestler. His original family name was Koki Naya.

Taiho won thirty-two of the most important tournaments, the Emperor's Cup, held six times each year, more than twice as many as any other sumo wrestler ever. In eight of these wins, his dominance was so complete that he did not lose a single one of the fifteen bouts that each wrestler must fight in the tournament. Taiho had his final victory in 1971, after which he retired.

▲ Taiho with the Emperor's Cup in 1961 after one of his first top wins. He was promoted to 'yokozuna' or 'grand champion' in the official rankings for this success. Taiho was the youngest-ever yokozuna.

▼ Taiho (centre) and other wrestlers perform the opening ceremonies before a tournament.

Foreigners in Japan's national sport
In recent years, a number of non-Japanese people, mostly from Pacific islands, have become well-known sumo wrestlers, and there was considerable debate in Japan as to whether they should qualify for the highest ranking titles in the sport.

Dawn Fraser
Australia, born 1937

Top swimmers tend to have a relatively brief career at the highest level of their sport, but Dawn Fraser was a brilliant exception to this rule. She is the only swimmer ever to have won the gold medal at her event (100 metres freestyle) at three successive Olympic games (1956, 1960 and 1964).

Altogether she set twenty-seven world records in her individual events, including eleven in the 100 metres freestyle. She set three world records in an hour in her various races at the 1960 Olympics. Her most notable achievement was to become the first woman ever to swim 100 metres in less than one minute. Her eventual best time of 58.9 seconds remained the world record for eight years.

▼ Dawn Fraser shows off all her power, style and determination in this picture of her training for the 1964 Olympics.

Fraser never got on well with the Australian team managers. At the 1964 Olympics she was caught stealing a souvenir from the Emperor's Palace in Tokyo and was banned for ten years by the Australian authorities. The Japanese did not really mind, and the ban was reduced, but she never competed seriously again.

Duncan Goodhew
Great Britain, born 1957

In the late 1970s and early 1980s, Duncan Goodhew was one of Britain's favourite sportsmen. He first came to international notice when he reached the 1976 Olympic Games finals in the 100 metres breaststroke. He was then still a schoolboy. Goodhew could only come seventh in that race, but his bald head had already been noticed as one to watch (he had become bald after a childhood accident and illness).

His greatest day was in the 1980 Moscow Olympics when he charged down the pool to take the 100 metres breaststroke gold. Goodhew said afterwards that all through his great race he thought he could hear his mum's voice cheering him on above all the noise that everyone else in the crowd was making.

▼ Many top swimmers wear caps so that their heads slip through the water easily, but that was one piece of special equipment Duncan Goodhew never needed!

The 1980 Olympic Boycott
Some nations did not compete in the 1980 Olympics (held in Moscow) in protest at the USSR's involvement in the war in Afghanistan. One sadness for Goodhew was that his stepfather, a retired senior Royal Air Force officer, did not come to watch Duncan swim, as part of his own personal protest.

Michael Gross
West Germany, born 1964

Michael Gross was one of the most successful and versatile swimmers competing during the 1980s.

By the 1982 world championships, Gross had reached the peak of his form, and won gold medals in both the 200 metres butterfly and freestyle. In the 1984 Olympics, he confirmed his status with wins in the 200 metres freestyle and 100 metres butterfly, both achieved in world-record times.

Gross successfully defended his two world championship titles in 1986 and in the 1988 Olympics won the 200 metres butterfly. He did this in the best possible style, taking the gold in a new Olympic record time.

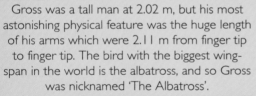

Gross was a tall man at 2.02 m, but his most astonishing physical feature was the huge length of his arms which were 2.11 m from finger tip to finger tip. The bird with the biggest wing-span in the world is the albatross, and so Gross was nicknamed 'The Albatross'.

▲ Michael Gross with one of the three European Championship gold medals he won in 1983. He won 13 golds in all in various European Championships.

▼ The Albatross spreads his 'wings' and powers ahead in another butterfly race.

Arthur Ashe
USA, 1943–93

Arthur Ashe was an African-American and is remembered for succeeding in a sport that before his time had been an almost completely white game.

Ashe had a successful sporting career at the University of California at Los Angeles, during which he was three times named as All-American and won the NCAA singles title in 1965.

After graduating, he served in the US Army and so at first did not play full-time tennis. In 1968, however, he won the US Open. He would later go on to win the Australian Open in 1970 and, his finest triumph of all, Wimbledon in 1975. In the Wimbledon final he beat the world number one and defending champion, Jimmy Connors.

▲ Arthur Ashe celebrating his 1975 Wimbledon success with the championship trophy.

▼ Arthur Ashe stretches for a backhand stroke during his Wimbledon final in 1975.

Throughout his life, Ashe was a notable campaigner against racism. As a boy he had been forbidden from playing in school tournaments in Virginia where he was born. Later he worked to improve civil rights throughout the USA, and against apartheid in South Africa. In the final years of his life, he also established a foundation to advance AIDS research.

Ashe was proud of his record in US Davis Cup teams. He won twenty-seven of his thirty-two Davis Cup singles and, after he stopped playing, was non-playing captain of the winning US team in 1981 and 1982. Ashe had to stop playing following a heart attack in 1979, and died in 1993 of an AIDS-related illness because he had been infected with HIV by a contaminated blood transfusion during heart surgery.

Björn Borg
Sweden, born 1956

Björn Borg was the man to beat at Wimbledon in the second half of the 1970s, but nobody did. The Swede holds the amazing record of winning the Wimbledon singles title five years in succession from 1976 to 1980.

The final in 1980 in which Borg beat one of his great rivals, the American John McEnroe, is said to have been one of the greatest matches of all time. They played five sets of superlative tennis with a nail-biting tie-break in the fourth set, which McEnroe won, only for Borg to make an astonishing come-back and take the final set 8–6.

Borg relied less on the serve and volley tactics used by most of the top

▼ ▶ Two pictures of Björn Borg during his 1979 Wimbledon singles success. Borg was one of the last top players to use the traditional wooden racket.

Borg led the Swedish team to his country's first-ever win in the Davis Cup in 1975, and he won thirty-seven out of the forty singles matches that he played in the Cup competitions.
His success also inspired later Swedish players to win the competition three times out of seven appearances in the final in the 1980s.

men, and instead cultivated fierce ground strokes including a powerful two-handed backhand. His strongest assets, however, were probably his total concentration and determination.

As well as his five Wimbledon titles, Borg also won the French Open a record six times, but never succeeded in the Australian Open or the US Open, where he lost in the final four times. He retired in 1983. However, he made a come-back in the early 1990s, but did not succeed.

Jimmy Connors
USA, born 1952

Jimmy Connors first made his mark on the world of tennis when he won the US Collegiate championship in 1971. He then joined the professional circuit and quickly became one of its stars.

Like his great rival for much of the 1970s, the Swede Björn Borg, Connors did not rely on the traditional serve and volley tactics of the other stars of the men's game. His ground strokes and return of service were his best shots, and he backed them up with all-out effort and a determination never to lose.

Connors was the world number one from 1974 to 1978, and won five of his total of eight top singles titles in these years. His best year was 1974 when he

▼ Jimmy Connors puts all his power into this two-handed backhand stroke during a match in the 1985 Wimbledon championships.

Fact File
World number one: 1974–8
Total weeks as number one: 268 (1974–83)
Wimbledon Champion: 1974, 1982
US Open Champion: 1975, 1976, 1982, 1983
Tournament wins: 109 singles titles
Career earnings: US $8,471,435

won the Australian, US and Wimbledon championships, and might have won the French title as well if he had not been stopped from playing in it because of an off-court dispute.

Connors had another period of good fortune in 1982–3, winning Wimbledon in 1982 and the US Open at Forest Hills in both of those years. He went on to play at the top level until 1992, often beating the younger players who had taken over as the best in the game.

Margaret Court
Australia, born 1942

By almost every measurement, Margaret Court was the best tennis player ever, man or woman. She was brought up in a small town in New South Wales in Australia, and as a youngster she played much of her tennis against men because they were the only available opponents who could give her a good game. She adopted the serve and volley style of play, and added to it speed around the court and natural athletic ability.

Court is one of only three women and two men to have won a Grand Slam of the top singles tournaments. She completed this feat in 1970, and won three out of the four major championships in an additional four years. She was also a top doubles player.

▲ The young Margaret Smith in action in 1963.

▼ Margaret Court during the Wimbledon leg of her great 1970 Grand Slam of the top singles titles.

Her win at Wimbledon in 1970 was one of her finest. Although she was hampered by an ankle injury and her opponent was the formidable Billie Jean King, Court won a marathon two-set victory 14–12, 11–9 (in those days, tie-breaks were not used).

Court competed at the top level from 1959 to 1977 and was known by her maiden name, Margaret Smith, until her marriage in 1967.

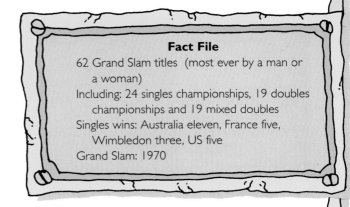

Fact File
62 Grand Slam titles (most ever by a man or a woman)
Including: 24 singles championships, 19 doubles championships and 19 mixed doubles
Singles wins: Australia eleven, France five, Wimbledon three, US five
Grand Slam: 1970

Steffi Graf
Germany, born 1969

Steffi Graf is one of only three women ever to have won a Grand Slam of tennis' top four singles tournaments, and even more sensationally she did it in 1988 when she was aged only nineteen.

Steffi first began really to be noticed in the summer of 1986, when she turned sixteen, and notched up wins over the two best players in the world, Chris Evert and Martina Navratilova. In 1987 she had her first big tournament success when she took the French Open singles title, beating Navratilova in the final.

Steffi is a strong and athletic player. Her backhand may sometimes be a little weak, but she makes up for it with her powerful and accurate forehand,

▲ Steffi Graf serves during the first round of the 1994 Wimbledon tournament.

▼ An unusual overhead shot of Steffi Graf serving during the 1994 US Open in which she lost in the final to Arantxa Sanchez Vicario.

In the four wins that made up her 1988 Grand Slam, Steffi showed her superiority over her top opponents. Chris Evert was beaten in Australia, Natalia Zvereva in France, Martina Navratilova at Wimbledon and Gabriela Sabatini at the US championships. Then Steffi went to Seoul and won the Olympics as well.

working opponents all round the court before passing them with a winning shot.

Women's tennis has seen many young stars come forward in recent years, just like Steffi, only for them to fade away after a brief period at the top. Steffi has proved to be different, winning at least one Grand Slam singles title in every year since her great triumphs of 1988.

Billie Jean King
USA, born 1943

Billie Jean King was a very courageous and attacking American player with a powerful serve and volley at the heart of her game – qualities that made her the world's number one from 1966 to 1974.

Her most successful championship was Wimbledon. She won the singles six times and added ten wins in the doubles and four in the mixed doubles for a total of 20 championships, the best by any player, man or woman. She won all three Wimbledon titles in 1967 and 1973.

King won other major tournaments, too. She won the singles at the US Open four times, and added one win each at the French and Australian championships. She never managed the

▼ Billie Jean King raises the Wimbledon ladies singles trophy high in delight after her win in the tournament in 1975.

The Battle of the Sexes
Billie Jean King won a famous match in 1973 against Bobbie Riggs. Riggs had been a top male player some years before and had begun challenging many of the best women players in exhibition matches.
He could not keep up with King, however, and she beat him in three straight sets.

elusive 'Grand Slam' of all four titles in a single year, but in 1972 she won three of them, losing out only in Australia.

Off the court, she worked hard for women's tennis. She was one of the leaders of the women's players' organizations, helping to improve the running of the game and bringing more prize money into it for women. King's maiden name was Billie Jean Moffitt, but she used her married name for most of her tennis career.

Martina Navratilova
Czechoslovakia/USA, born 1956

Martina Navratilova was the dominant figure in women's tennis for most of the 1980s. She was born and raised in Czechoslovakia and had her first tennis successes as a Czech, reaching the Wimbledon and Australian finals in 1975. Later that year she went to live in the USA, eventually becoming a US citizen in 1981.

Navratilova was a tall and powerful left-hander who brought new standards of fitness to the women's game. She won eighteen major championship singles titles, including a record nine at Wimbledon.

Her last appearance in the singles at Wimbledon was in 1994, when tennis fans everywhere hoped she might win a record tenth title, but she lost in the final to Conchita Martinez of Spain.

▲ Martina Navratilova at the French championships in 1986. She only won the French title once, in 1984.

The Federation Cup

The Federation Cup is the top team competition in international women's tennis. Navratilova holds the unique distinction of being on the winning side in the Federation Cup for two different countries. She was a member of the Czech team that won in 1975, and of the US teams of 1982, 1986, and 1989.

▼ Navratilova at Wimbledon in 1990 when she won the last of her nine singles titles.

Pete Sampras
USA, born 1971

In 1995 Pete Sampras was nothing less than the best tennis player in the world. He first reached the number one position in the world rankings in 1993, and has stayed there virtually continuously ever since.

Sampras turned professional in 1988 and started a steady progression to the top. By 1993, he was contesting the top place with the US player Jim Courier, and wins at Wimbledon and in the US Open saw Sampras edge ahead.

Sampras's first major win was in the US Open in 1990, just a few days after his nineteenth birthday. That made him the youngest-ever winner of this Grand Slam title.

▼ Pete Sampras seems to be all concentration and poise in this picture taken during the 1994 US Open, but he lost surprisingly in the fourth round.

Sampras has the ability to play all the strokes in the game well, with powerful serving backed by superb volleying and ground strokes. Some people say he is so good that his matches are boring. Perhaps Sampras is happy to put up with this reputation considering the US $16,500,000 he had won by 1995.

In 1994 he achieved ten wins, including the Australian and Wimbledon titles. Sampras is at his best on the lightning-quick grass courts, but in 1994 his tournament successes were achieved on all four of the types of court used by the top players. In 1995, Sampras added a third successive Wimbledon title, which ranks him among the best in the history of the tournament.

Virginia Wade
Great Britain, born 1945

Virginia Wade is remembered as a rare British success at Britain's own tennis championships, Wimbledon.

Wade first played at Wimbledon in 1962 and went on to compete in the championships a record twenty-five times. She soon made herself a favourite of the Wimbledon crowds, and a force to be reckoned with in women's tennis. She won the US Open singles title at Forest Hills in 1968, and added the Australian title to her list of successes in 1972.

She was also a very good doubles player, winning three of the four top tournaments with Margaret Court in 1973. They did not play together at

▼ One of the best parts of Virginia Wade's game was her volleying. She really has to stretch out for this one during her 1977 Wimbledon win.

Wade and Team Tennis
Wade played in fifty-seven Federation Cup matches, more than any player ever, and in more Wightman Cup matches between Britain and the US than any other player. One record Wade could not match was achieved by the US player Chris Evert. She won all twenty-six of her Wightman Cup singles matches.

Wimbledon in that year or they might well have completed a doubles Grand Slam. She also won the US doubles title in 1975 (again with Court).

The hundredth birthday, or centenary, of the Wimbledon championships was celebrated in 1977, and everyone in Britain hoped there would be a home success at the tournament. Wade delighted the fans when she won a famous singles victory, beating the Dutch player Betty Stove in the final by two sets to one.

Mark Allen
USA, born 1958

All champion sportsmen and women have to put in many hours of training to achieve success in their various events, but possibly the most difficult of all events is the triathlon. Triathletes must complete three long races one after another in a single day: a swim is followed by a cycle ride and, to complete the competition, a long run.

The distances for these various sections vary between competitions, but for the most famous event of all, the Hawaii Ironman Championships, they are a 3.9-km swim, followed by a 180-km cycle ride and then finally a full marathon run of 42.2 km. For many competitors it is enough simply to finish the course!

▼ The number one on the runner's chest says it all. This is Mark Allen in 1991 in the middle of his sequence of Hawaii Ironman wins.

Women in the Hawaii Triathlon
South Africa's Paula Newby-Fraser has won the women's event in Hawaii seven times. Her record for the course is 8 hours 55 minutes 28 seconds set in 1992, a time which would have been good enough to win the men's race in each year from 1978 to 1983.

The Hawaii race starts at 7.00 am and the course is kept open to midnight to give the slower finishers a chance just to complete the race. The record time is an astonishing 8 hours 7 minutes 45 seconds. That record was set by one of triathlon's finest ever exponents, Mark Allen, when he won the race for the fifth year in succession in 1993.

Allen was also the first ever men's triathlon world champion (over a shorter course than in Hawaii) when that event was first held in 1989.

Roger Bannister

Great Britain, born 1929

Roger Bannister is famous for an achievement on a single day, in an event that is not even contested very regularly in the modern world. The day was 6 May 1954 and the location was the Oxford University athletics field at Iffley Road in Oxford.

In athletics, targets in achievement are continually being set which are finally reached and surpassed. After the Second World War (1939–45), one target was thought to be impossible – to run a mile in under four minutes. But as the 1950s began, it seemed that this was in sight.

▲ Roger Bannister about to cross the finish line.

On the big day Bannister ran a great race but had he broken the record? The crowd held their breaths for the announcement of the winning time, but as soon as the announcer said 'three minutes' they did not need to let him finish for they knew already that the record had been achieved.

Bannister and Landy

Bannister's great rival was an Australian, John Landy. Later in 1954 they ran in the first-ever mile race in which two men both beat four minutes. The current world mile record is 3 minutes 44.39 seconds, and was set by Noureddine Morceli of Algeria in 1993.

▼ An exhausted Roger Bannister waits for that special announcement.

Abebe Bikila
Ethiopia, 1932–73

Abebe Bikila came to the 1960 Olympic Games in Rome having run in only two marathons (a distance of 42.195 kilometres) in his native Ethiopia. He was a soldier and had only begun running competitively after he joined the Ethiopian army when he was already grown up.

At Rome he surprised all the experts by not only winning the marathon, but doing so in what was then the world record-breaking time of 2 hours 15 minutes 16.2 seconds.

The next Olympic Games were at Tokyo in 1964, and Bikila came back to defend his marathon title. He became the only man to do this successfully, coming home in front in a time of 2 hours 12 minutes 11.2 seconds, which was again the best-ever recorded to that date.

What was the difference between Bikila's two Olympic marathon wins? For the second one in 1964, he wore shoes! Remarkably his first Olympic success in 1960, in this longest and most punishing of races, was achieved barefoot.

▼ ▶ Abebe Bikila during his two Olympic marathon wins. At Rome in 1960 he runs barefoot (above). At Tokyo in 1964, he wears shoes (below).

Fanny Blankers-Koen
Netherlands, born 1918

Fanny Blankers-Koen is best remembered for her performance at the 1948 Olympic Games, held in London. She was the world record holder in both the high and long jumps, but did not even compete in these events. Instead, she devoted herself to the track and still ended up with four gold medals from one Olympics, a record that has not been beaten by any other woman in the history of track and field.

Her gold medal performances were achieved in the 100 metres, 200 metres, 80 metres hurdles and the 4 by 100 metres relay. She was even more versatile than this record suggests. During her career, she held world records in eight different events, including all those already mentioned and the 100 yards sprint and the five-event competition, the pentathlon.

▲ Fanny Blankers-Koen crosses the finishing line to win the 200m at the 1948 Olympics.

Four-time Gold Medal Winners

Only three other track and field athletes have equalled Blankers-Koen's feat of winning four Olympic gold medals, but none at one Olympic Games. They are Betty Cuthbert of Australia (1956 and 1964), Barbel Eckert Wöckel of East Germany (1976 and 1980), and Evelyn Ashford of the USA (1984 and 1992).

▼ Blankers-Koen (nearest the camera) early in her winning 80m hurdles race in 1948.

Sergei Bubka
USSR/Ukraine, born 1963

Most top sports stars have a number of close challengers in their events, but occasionally a sport has a single superstar who is so far ahead of all the rest as to be just about unbeatable. Sergei Bubka is one of these rare people.

Bubka surprised everyone when he won the pole vault in the 1983 World Championships. Since this, his first major win, the only real surprise in a pole vault competition was in the 1992 Olympics when he had three failures at his opening heights and was out of the competition. Otherwise he has been supreme.

His first world record came outdoors in 1983, and he has improved his outdoor or his indoor mark at least once every year since then. His current world indoor and outdoor records are both a massive 30 cm higher than when he began competing.

▼ Pole vaulters must achieve a special combination of speed in their run up with strength and technique to control the pole and the jump. Sergei Bubka is the best there has ever been.

Bubka's World Records
Bubka has set more world records in a single event than anyone else, but people wonder how often he has been trying his hardest. Bonuses are often given to athletes for new world records and some fans suggest that Bubka has deliberately beaten his own records a little bit at a time to keep earning this extra money.

Linford Christie
Great Britain, born 1960

Before Linford Christie, everyone used to say that sprinting was a young person's sport, and that anyone over 30 years of age was past their best. Christie has repeatedly proved this to be wrong.

Christie has not set many record times in his career, although his best ever of 9.87 seconds for the 100 metres is only two-thousandths of a second outside the current world record. Instead, he has become known for his ability to produce the winning performance in the very biggest events.

Christie's best season was probably in 1992 when he won thirteen out of sixteen of the major races he ran in, including an all-important Olympic gold medal performance and a World Cup win. He confirmed his superiority in 1993 with a win in the World Championship.

▶ Christie leads a British relay team in 1994.

▼ Power and concentration, Christie wins again.

Despite all his wins in major championship events, Christie had to wait until 1995 when he was 35 years old to set his first world record. At a meeting in France in February that year, he set a new indoor mark for 200 metres of 20.25 seconds.

Jackie Joyner-Kersee
USA, born 1962

Jackie Joyner-Kersee is one of the greatest-ever all-round track and field athletes. Her special skill is the heptathlon, in which points are scored in seven events, over two days of competition. The seven events are: 100 metres, high jump, shot putt, 200 metres, long jump, javelin, and 800 metres.

Joyner-Kersee has simply been the best in the world at this complicated range of skills since the mid-1980s. She won the Olympic gold medal in 1988 with a score of 7,291 points, which is still the world record. She won the Olympic heptathlon again in 1992 and was also world champion in 1987 and 1993.

Joyner-Kersee has also been a formidable competitor in individual events. In the long jump she won Olympic gold in 1988 and the world championship in 1987, 1991 and 1993.

▼ Joyner-Kersee during the javelin section of the 1987 heptathlon World Championship, her first world championship win.

Joyner-Kersee's brother, Al Joyner, won the gold medal in the triple jump in the 1984 Olympics. His wife, Florence Griffith-Joyner (known as Flo-Jo), did even better. She won gold medals in the 100 metres, 200 metres and sprint relay at the 1988 Olympics, as well as a silver medal in the 4 by 400 metres relay.

Marita Koch
East Germany, born 1957

Marita Koch was probably the world's best-ever woman sprinter. The 400 metres was her finest event, but she was almost as good at the 200 metres and 100 metres. She retired from competition in 1986, and the world record she set at 400 metres in 1985 – 47.60 seconds – has not even been threatened since then.

Koch was more than just good at setting records. She could also produce her best performances in the top competitions. From 1978 until she retired in 1986, she was beaten only twice in the 400 metres, and altogether won 17 gold medals at her various distances. She was Olympic 400 metres champion in 1980.

When the World Championships were started in 1983, she won the 200 metres, along with a silver medal in the 100 metres.

▼ Marita Koch (in blue) races in 1977 against one of her great rivals Irina Szewinska of Poland. Szewinska won this race in a world record time, but it was the last time Marita Koch lost a 400m race for four years.

Drugs in Athletics
Koch competed for the former communist country of East Germany. There are many stories of how the East Germans made their athletes take illegal drugs. Koch was never found to have taken drugs, but some people believe that all the records set by East Germans in those years have been put in doubt.

Carl Lewis
USA, born 1961

Carl Lewis was one of the finest-ever long jumpers and sprinters. His eight gold medals put him far ahead of any modern competitor in the Olympic medal table, and he has also won eight World Championship golds as well.

Lewis's best championship was the 1984 Olympics when he won the gold in all four of his events (long jump, 100 and 200 metres and 4 by 100 metres relay).

In the 100 metres, Lewis set the world record twice and his best time of 9.86 seconds has only been improved by one-hundredth of a second. That was by Leroy Burrell of the USA in 1994.

In the 1988 Olympics 100 metres, Canadian runner Ben Johnson crossed the line first in the incredible time of 9.79 seconds, well clear of Lewis who was in second place. Afterwards, Johnson was discovered to have cheated by taking illegal performance-enhancing drugs, and his medal and records were awarded to Lewis.

▲ Lewis was unbeaten in long jump competitions from 1981 to 1991, including here at the 1988 Olympics in Seoul where he took the gold medal.

▼ Carl Lewis (left) celebrates his win in the 1984 Olympic Games 100 metres in front of his home fans in Los Angeles.

Jesse Owens
USA, 1913-80

Some athletes who participate in track and field events have been versatile enough to set records in a range of different events. One day in May 1935, Jesse Owens went one better than this. He became the only man ever to set a track and a field record on the same day, and the only man ever to set six world records in that one day also, in fact gaining them all within one hour.

The 1936 Olympics were held in the German capital, Berlin. The Nazi dictator of Germany, Adolf Hitler, wanted to use the games to 'prove' his racist theories, but instead Jesse Owens showed that such ideas were nonsense.

Owens won one team and three individual gold medals, two of them in world record times. Hitler was furious, but Jesse Owens came home in triumph.

▼ Jesse Owens winning one of his four 1936 gold medals. He took gold in the 100m, 200m, long jump, and, as part of the US team, in the sprint relay.

Owens and Long
One of the reasons Hitler was so angry at Owens' win in the long jump was that the German athlete, Luz Long, was strongly favoured for a medal. Although Hitler would have disapproved, Long helped Owens in the preliminary rounds of the event, so that Owens was able to get into the final.

Babe Zaharias
USA, 1911-56

Babe Zaharias was a brilliant all-round sportswoman. She was an All-American basketball player in the early 1930s, and played in exhibition matches against the top male baseball players later in that decade. However, these sporting successes pale against her achievements in track and field.

In the 1932 Olympics, women were only allowed to enter three events. From her widely ranging choices, Babe won gold medals in the 80 metres hurdles and the javelin, and a silver in the high jump!

She was probably even better as a golfer. Her professional titles included the US Women's Open in 1948, 1950, and 1954. She was one of the founders of the Ladies Professional Golf Association.

▼ Mrs Zaharias wins the 1947 British Women's golf championship, when she was still an amateur player.

▲ It's 1932 and no one can catch Mildred Didrikson.

Zaharias's original name was Mildred Didrikson. She earned her nickname, 'Babe', in imitation of the great baseball player, Babe Ruth.
To complete her sporting connections, in later life she married an American professional wrestler, George Zaharias, and is now usually remembered by her married name.

Look for the words on the ball in the grid formed by the strings of the racquet. Words may read up, down or diagonally. Some letters are used more than once, although never twice in the same word.

There are **34 WORDS** in the Racquet

Word list:

MEXICO TEN
CREW SEVE THICKEN
INDIAN NECK ANSWERS
WRONG BOYS ENGLAND
HELPED SKEW SWING
ELEVATED PROFESSIONALLY
ELECTION EDWARDS IDEAL
SMIRNOVA SAMPRAS SERVE
INFECTED DESPITE SOLE
KNOCK SUCCESS GOLF
JUMPS MANCHESTER
ARNOLD SIEGES
LET AIM

Answers can be found on page 111

108

Index

Picture Acknowledgements

t = top; b = below

Allsport: 13t, 16b, 18t, cover & 18b, 20t, 24t, 24b, 26t, cover & 40t, 40b, 49, 71b, 72b, 77t, 82b, 86b, 90t, 90b, 91b, 92t, 92b, 93t, cover & 93b, 94t, 96t, 99b, 100t, 100b, 104t, 106b.
Allsport/Hulton Deutsch: 29t, 29b, 31t, 6 & 31b, 32b, 37t, 42t, 42b, 7 & 48, 51b, 63b, 71t, 72t, 73t, 73b, 74t, 74b, 79t, 79b, 84t, cover & 84b, 88t, 88b, 91t, cover & 98t, 98b, 99t, 106t, 107b.

Allsport/Inpho: 70t.
Allsport/MSI: cover & 70b.
Allsport/Agence Vandystadt: 26b.
Allsport/individuals: Bruno Bade 28t; Shaun Botterill 59, 75t; Clive Brunskill 68t, 95t, 95b, 68b; Simon Bruty 76t, 83t, cover & 105t; David Cannon 41t, 43b, 44t, 45t, 45b, 46t, 46b, 47t, 47b, cover & 66t, 66b, 69t, 76b, 77b, 82t, 83b; Graham Chadwick 34b; Russell Cheyne cover & 60t, 60b, 61b, 62t, 62b; Chris Cole cover & 27b, 64t, 78b; Glenn Cratty 53t; J.D. Cuban 41b, 53b; Jonathan Daniel 9t, 20b,
22b; Tim Defrisco 25b, cover, 6 & 56t, 56b; Steve Dopaola 25t; Tony Duffy 23b, cover & 50b, 50t, 57b, 57t, cover, 1 & 58b, 58t, 86t, 87t, 89b, 96b, cover & 102t, 103b, 104b; Mike Dunn 21b; Stephen Dunn 21t; Stuart Forster 38t; John Gichigi 39t; Michael King cover & 87b; David Leah 78t; Bob Martin 64b, 94b; Don Morley 43t; Gary Mortimore 67t, cover & 101b, 102t, 102b; Stephen Munday 39b; Adrian Murrell cover & 30t, 30b, 33t, 33b, 35; Gary Newkirk 97t, 97b; Mike Powell 28b, 101t; Steve Powell 44b, 89t,
105b; Ben Radford cover & 34t, 35t, 36t, 36b, 38b, 75b; Dave Rogers 61t; Pascal Rondeau 27t, cover, 7 & 67b; Rick Stewart 23t; Damian Strohmeyer 19t, 19b; Claudio Villa 69b; Anton Want cover & 52.
Associated Press: 85b.
Corbis-Bettmann/UPI: 8, 9b, 10t, 10b, 11t, 6 & 11b, 12t, 12b, 13b, 15t, 15b, 16t, 17t, 17b, 54, 107t.
Hulton Deutsch Collection: 51t, 85t.
Pica Pressfoto AB: 55t, 55b.
Popperfoto: 14t, cover & 14b, 32t, 37t, 63t, 65t, 65b, cover & 80t, 80b, 81t, 81b